MANUAL OF MANAGEMENT DEVELOPMENT

MANUAL OF MANAGEMENT DEVELOPMENT

Strategy, Design and Instruments for Programme Improvement

JOHN E. JONES and MIKE WOODCOCK

Gower

The materials that appear in this book, other than those quoted from prior sources, may be reproduced for educational/training activities. There is no requirement to obtain special permission for such uses. We do, however, ask that the following statement appear on all reproductions.

> Reproduced from the *Manual of Management Development* by John E. Jones and Mike Woodcock. Aldershot, England: Gower, 1985.

This permission statement is limited to reproduction of materials for educational or training events. Systematic or large-scale reproduction or distribution – or inclusion of items in publication for sale – may be done only with prior written permission.

Published by
Gower Publishing Company Limited,
Gower House,
Croft Road,
Aldershot,
Hants GU11 3HR,
England.

Gower Publishing Company,
Old Post Road,
Brookfield,
Vermont 05036,
U.S.A.

British Library Cataloguing in Publication Data

Jones, John E.
　　Manual of management development.
　　1. Management
　　I. Title　II. Woodcock, Mike
　　658.4　　HD31

ISBN 0-566-02527-2

Typeset in Great Britain by
Guildford Graphics Limited, Plaistow, West Sussex.
Printed and bound in Great Britain by
Redwood Burn Limited, Trowbridge, Wiltshire.

Contents

Foreword

by   The Rt Hon Tom King MP
     Secretary of State for Employment

In recent years we have witnessed an ever-increasing rate of change in our business and commercial life, as well as the service sectors of our economy. We look to managers to provide the foresight, planning, organisational and leadership skills which each enterprise needs to meet its ever changing market.

Good management does not just happen, it has to be worked for, with each member of the team learning from both their own, and their colleagues' mistakes. Although the very act of managing is a learning process, successful managements do their best to 'get it right first time', and this requires management learning to take place before the critical performance activities begin. No business stands still and success requires a continuous approach to the development of managers.

John Jones and Mike Woodcock have drawn heavily on their own experience in developing managers to write this manual. Though it is designed as a guide for management development specialists, its many useful themes and practical exercises should assist other practising managers to find new ways to review and improve their managerial competence.

Preface

This book came out of discussions that the two authors had while both were associated with University Associates. As colleagues in that organisation, we had many occasions to compare our perceptions of how management development is practised in the UK and in America. We decided to develop these discussions into the present Manual by pooling our experiences and studying the subject through the available literature. Hence, we extended our contacts with each other, and this 'hands-across-the-sea' approach led to many fruitful hours of comparing the samenesses and differences in how people develop organisational leadership in the two situations. Of course, we found many more samenesses than differences, and this publication represents our considered judgement about the best practices.

The Manual is intended to be used as a guide for management development specialists. These professionals may call themselves trainers, facilitators, human resource development practitioners, or consultants. We have included not only theory about management but also step-by-step methods that can be used to set up and improve management-development programmes.

A unique feature of the Manual is the inclusion of a series of instruments that can be reproduced and used within management development schemes. The paper-and-pencil questionnaires are designed to be immediately useful in planning, designing, and delivering high-quality learning experiences for organisational leadership.

In a sense this Manual represents what the two of us have learned in a combined thirty-five years of helping to develop managers. We have spent countless hours and days planning, designing, and delivering experientially-focused learning experiences for leaders and those who show leadership potential. There is a lot of *us* in this manual – our strongly held points of view as well as our biases about hard-hitting, practical training.

We want to thank three people who helped us in developing the Manual. Laura Jones assisted in the library research. Angela O'Donoghue's administrative help was invaluable in all phases of the writing project. Colleen Kelley reacted to several drafts of the chapters. Our clients were most understanding in permitting us to conduct experimental tryouts of the various instruments.

HOW TO USE THIS MANUAL

Chapter 1 presents a broad overview of management development and two reproducible instruments that can assist in setting priorities for programme improvement. In Chapter 2 we define a model of managerial competencies and challenges for leadership effectiveness. Chapter 3 focuses on training needs assessment, with practical suggestions for strategy and tools to assist in the process. Since we are emphasising training in this manual, Chapter 4 includes what we have learned about how to design events so that they are participative and effective. In Chapter 5 we cover logistical planning in conducting experiential training. Since the best design can be wrecked by poor trainer behaviour, Chapter 6 lays out our guidance on facilitator style. The remaining chapter is concerned with evaluating training.

This Manual has been developed for several purposes, among which are:

1 Guidance for programme development;
2 Assessment of current programme adequacy;
3 Redesign of courses;
4 Evaluation of outcomes of current courses;
5 Enrichment of existing offerings;
6 'Fixing' problematic areas in current programmes;
7 Providing new ideas for strategy, tactics, and techniques.

The Manual can be used in numerous ways. It should be studied thoroughly before any of its main ideas are implemented. An organisational training staff and its management development advisory committee can use the book for programme self-assessment purposes. It can also serve as a reference for ideas and resources. External consultants may find much of the material helpful in evaluating programmes and designing and evaluating training events. Persons applying for management development positions can use the materials in this manual to determine what kind of programme they are about to join.

A step-by-step developmental sequence for using this book is suggested below. Of course, the steps would have to be adapted to local conditions and practices.

1   Conduct an assessment of the present programme using the MDAA and the MDA.
2   Study the managerial competencies model in Chapter 2.
3   Conduct a training needs assessment in accordance with guidelines in Chapter 3.
4   Design/redesign courses, using data from the needs assessment principles laid out in Chapter 4.
5   Conduct the courses, including soliciting feedback on trainer style, as suggested in Chapter 5.
6   Schedule the new and revamped training events, keeping in mind the considerations in Chapter 6.
7   Evaluate the outcomes of the courses according to methods outlined in Chapter 7.
8   Repeat the entire process.

This sequence usually takes over a year to implement, but that should not discourage trainers from doing it. It is an educational process. Not only will the programme benefit from such methodical developments, but also trainers will learn and grow as well.

John E. Jones
Mike Woodcock

1 Management development overview

This book is intended to be used as a manual or reference work for management development specialists. Included in the various chapters are training and development instruments which can be used to obtain relevant information to improve and extend existing management development courses or to design new ones.

Management development is an ambiguous term, so we shall define what we mean by it. Actually, we found in the British literature a satisfactory definition. Denning, Hussey, and Newman (1978) state:

> We define Management Development as the total process which an organization adopts in preparing its managers for the growth and change that occur in their working environment. (p. 6)

So we shall use the term management development in this book to mean 'the sum of all the activities available to individuals to help them to meet their growth needs and keep the organisation viable'. As we shall discuss later, this encompasses both formal, systematic programmes, and informal, on-the-job opportunities – a wide array of processes.

This book will not directly address organisation development (OD) even though this activity is closely related to and supportive of management development. The technology of OD is applied to system problems, and the system itself is considered the 'client'. In management development the individual is the client, and system development is effected by increasing the competencies of individual managers. As we shall point out in Chapter 4, we believe that it is desirable to make a sharp distinction between these two types of programme, although we do believe that it is desirable for organisations to engage in both. Most organisations do not have sufficient OD readiness (Pfeiffer & Jones, 1978) to let that process be effective, but all organisations can profitably engaged in some form of management development.

Our specific focus will be on in-house training as the most important vehicle for management development. This activity forms the bulk of most programmes, and we want to provide step-by-step methods for ensuring that the organisation's management training:

1   Meets real needs;
2   Is designed properly;
3   Is carried out with appropriate trainer behaviour;
4   Is evaluated carefully;
5   Is cost effective.

There is a need for a systematic approach to assessing and meeting management development needs, and this book provides such a system.

Many management development programmes are created without any obviously coherent plan. Sometimes they are expanded through opportunity or through the visions of training managers. In our judgement it is best to begin with a model of competent managerial behaviour and to devise developmental activities from that model. Since there has been greater emphasis on competency in recent years, we felt that it would be advantageous to concentrate on this aspect of management development. We could have taken the traditional categories of knowledge, skill, and attitude, but we wanted to focus primarily on effectiveness. The term 'competency' in our view subsumes knowledge, skill, and attitude and implies effectiveness. So our approach to management development centres around challenges to competency.

Almost everyone is familiar with the concept of the 'Peter Principle': people tend to rise to their level of incompetence within organisations. Management development should prevent this principle from operating, but it often does not. It is our belief that development that proceeds from coherent policy, that is tied to effective performance appraisal, that views incompetence as a problem requiring investigation and that involves employees in activities that they see as personally meaningful can prevent the Peter Principle from operating. The Peter Principle is a pessimistic, sarcastic notion, but management development is optimistic and forward-looking.

This chapter outlines the most common activities included in management development programmes, pointing out the potential assets and liabilities of each. We then turn our attention to the characteristics of effective and ineffective programmes, and we include a reproducible instrument for 'auditing' management development.

ESSENTIAL PROGRAMME FEATURES

In his study of management development programmes in 'well-managed' companies in the United States, Digman (1978) concluded that there is no universal way to develop managers. He found that companies conduct very successful management development programmes with company-unique approaches. There are, however, common elements that are included in many programmes. We shall look at the pros and cons of each of the essential programme features.

In-house training

This is probably the most common management development activity. This feature includes all courses organised and conducted internally within the organisation. The trainers may be internal and/or external, but the participants are almost always employees of the organisation.

The chief assets of in-house training are that:

1   It develops in-company knowledge and skills;
2   It helps to establish and maintain an organisational culture that supports formal norms and policy;
3   It is useful with geograhically dispersed units;
4   The training is (supposedly) tailored to the here-and-now and future needs of the organisation;
5   The curriculum (presumably) flows directly from the purposes of the organisation;
6   An 'ethos' is created within the system.

On the other hand, in-house training can become in-bred training. As Foy (1979) found in British companies:

> though the underlying purpose of such courses is often to reinforce a company ethos (and thus a company language) few are as company-specific as their members or designers presume.

The programme can pass along the organisation's mythology about how managers should behave, rather than testing its assumptions. Often in-house training is not so organisation-specific as it is made out to be. Management trainers bring in packaged training without adapting it to the unique demands of their organisation.

External training

This programme feature can include many practices. It involves sending employees to outside courses for training that the organisation cannot mount internally. This may mean academic degree programmes, public workshops, clinics, seminars, and conferences, and 'continuing education' courses. In this training the organisation's employees are grouped with people from other organisations, and the trainers are external to the organisation.

Advantages of external training that are most often mentioned by training managers are:

1 It promotes increased sensitivity to events in the organisation's external environment that affect the functioning of the system;
2 It helps employees to develop themselves personally in ways that would be too threatening if the training were conducted internally;
3 It provides a cross-cultural impact for employees;
4 It helps to bridge the gap between organisations;
5 It brings in new ideas and approaches;
6 It helps the organisation to challenge its assumptions.

The disadvantages of external training are:

1 It may not be directly relevant to the particular problems facing the organisation;
2 It is often expensive in terms of both time and money;
3 It may simply be fashionable ('Japanese Management, one more time') rather than usable;

4 It is often seen as a holiday or a reward rather than task-focused learning;
5 It is often difficult to apply in the organisation;
6 It sometimes creates barriers in the organisation.

Training centres

These are places managed by the training department, where the bulk of management training takes place. Often, these centres include living-in accommodation, or they are located near hotels and restaurants. They usually house the offices of members of the management development staff. They commonly feature extensive audiovisual aids, duplication facilities, and rooms designed especially for training.

Organisations that are well managed, according to Digman (1978), tend to operate their own training centres. The primary benefits of this practice are:

1 It facilitates the full development of in-house training capabilities;
2 It provides maximum control over the training site and schedule;
3 It highlights training as a legitimate activity within the organisation;
4 It has the potential of keeping expenses under control;
5 It can become a forum for ideas, materials, and expertise for management development within the organisation.

Training centres have their drawbacks, too. They must be used frequently in order to be cost effective. Empty training rooms and dormitory accommodations are expensive. Centres can become empires, fighting for their existence and expansion with the same sort of politics that management development seeks to obviate. They become 'ivory towers', in much the same way that many universities have developed. Operating a training centre can be an organisational burden, especially when the pressure is for the trainers to fill up seats rather than to meet real needs. Such places require day-to-day management, and this distracts trainers from their primary professional mission. Apart from this, many trainers are not effective managers. Training centres sometimes keep the training staff isolated from the mainstream of the organisation's activity, and this condition may make their courses less useful. The trainers may be seen as insufficiently aware of what is really going on within the system. Finally, the existence of a training centre may add to the travel expense associated with training in a geographically dispersed organisation.

Performance review

This involves regularly scheduled appraisals of employee job performance. This is a management development activity when it generates growth plans for individuals who are preparing for or who are already involved in the supervision of others' work. Reviews are ordinarily held annually, and they often form the basis of the organisation's succession planning process. Individuals are ideally guided in this activity toward higher levels of competence and responsibility. The data generated in performance review are sometimes made available to those persons who make decisions about individuals and to those who are involved in human-resource planning.

The advantages of a good performance review system are:

1   It provides for individual goal setting;
2   It improves boss-subordinate communications and relationships,
3   It provides the basis for effective career planning and guidance;
4   It puts the manager in the position of developing employees.

In our experience performance reviews are carried out less than satisfactorily in almost all organisations. As Pfeiffer (1979) points out:

> Most managers perceive performance appraisal as an interruption of their work. They view it as an exercise that has no relationship to the reason for which they are doing it. And when they are forced to do it – and perhaps this is most important from the HRD point of view – they do it without the necessary skills to make it effective. One of the reasons that the traditional system does not work is that it is almost always done on an anniversary basis linked to date of hire. (p. 317)

Reviews are often dishonest; managers use the old military rating tactic of 'damning with faint praise'. The review process can become bureaucratic and time-consuming. Reviews are sometimes perfunctory, carried out without any serious data-gathering or planning.

Amazingly, many appraisals are not goal-oriented, focusing only on how well the employee performed during the past year. When performance reviews are confused with salary reviews, appraisees often do not listen productively to feedback, since they are waiting to see what they will get in the way of rewards.

Career development

Usually this is a programme that features a counselling and information service to enable employees to manage their own careers within the organisation. This may involve courses, private consultations, vocational testing, and job vacancy advertising. It may simply be a responsibility of the individual manager.

The advantages of career development programmes are many. They help employees to develop responsibility in self management. Such activities can provide data to training managers for overall management development. Career development gives individuals and their managers the information they need to ensure that they are properly employed (neither under- nor over-employed). Perhaps most important, this activity puts pressure on managers to develop their subordinates.

Some potential liabilities of career development programmes are:

1 They can raise false expectations on the part of employees;
2 They can prepare people for opportunities that vanish during economically hard times;
3 They can lead to dissatisfaction and seeking alternative employment;
4 They can put more emphasis on individual development than on organisational needs.

Job rotation

This involves shifting managers and potential managers systematically through various jobs to develop skills and technical expertise. The advantages of job rotation are that:

1 It can give employees wide experience;
2 It can generate a sense of perspectiveness and 'worldliness' in the positive sense;
3 It can help managers gain new ideas, skills, and expertise;

4   It can have the effect of challenging the accepted order, or 'the way things are done around here';
5   It can generate interdepartmental crossfertilisation.

Some potential disadvantages are:

1   It requires that individuals make frequent, often stressful job adjustments;
2   It can interfere with the ongoing processes of the organisation;
3   It may result in individuals' coping more than learning;
4   It may not produce a 'helicopter' perspective (seeing both forest and trees);
5   It is often seen as a threat and/or nuisance by managers who are constantly taking on new people.

Secondments

This term is better known in the United Kingdom than in the United States. It refers to temporary assignments, usually within other organisations. This could include management being 'loaned out' to other systems such as the government, or executives serving for periods as line managers.

The utility of secondments, or temporary external job assignments include the following:

1   The cross-pollination of ideas;
2   An influx of skills can be effected where they are needed;
3   They can have a cross-cultural impact;
4   The potential for rapid problem solving in the host organisation;
5   Development of the 'helicopter' view.

Secondments, however, are not all positive experiences. Often they are met with resistance on both sides. They generate entry/re-entry problems. They are frequently viewed administratively as a nuisance. People are given inappropriate assignments, and they perform what amount to thankless tasks within the host organisation.

International assignments

These are a special kind of secondment, to organisations across national boundaries. They have all of the advantages discussed above and in addition they may help to foster better international understanding and contacts. Unfortunately they often have the same disadvantages as domestic secondments, in addition to language/cultural difficulties, added expense, and learning that may not be applicable back home. International assignments may be seen as a reward, vacation, or 'perk'.

Using consultants

This management development practice involves bringing in outside trainers to run courses, help design programmes, and assist in the evaluation of programme practices.

Outside trainers are useful because:

1   They can be employed to expand internal resources for management development;
2   They often bring new ideas and fresh approaches into the organisation;
3   They can challenge current management practices since they tend to be more confrontive than internal trainers;
4   They have no vested interest in how managers behave and can give their best professional judgements;
5   They can help to train internal trainers and lend them credibility;
6   They can be scheduled flexibly;
7   They often have access to executives that internal trainers cannot effectively influence;
8   They can bring objectivity to the evaluation of management development programmes.

There are dangers in using outside trainers, however. They can be insensitive to the nuances of the organisational culture. They are often expensive. They usually have little or no ongoing responsibility within the organisation. Sometimes they circumvent, rather than support the internal training staff. They may foster dependency in order to generate follow-on business. Sometimes they have 'a solution in search of a problem', and occasionally they are little more than entertainers.

Mentoring

This term, and practice, is more widely used in the United States than in the United Kingdom. It refers to the practice of assigning more senior managers to assist new managers to grow into their jobs. Sometimes mentors sit in on their charges' performance reviews. In some organisations mentors are given special training to fulfil this role.

The utility of mentoring programmes are:

1   They involve senior management in one-to-one developmental activities;
2   They can provide practical guidance for the 'mentees';
3   They may improve performance review systems;
4   They can open up communications from top management downwards;
5   They can provide 'godfather' assistances to individuals;
6   They can make provisions for ombudsman services.

The problems of mentoring are:

1   They take expensive senior management time;
2   They may generate insubordination;
3   They can inadvertently elicit jealousy by putting 'mentees' into a kind of favoured-person status.

Counselling

This management development activity consists of offering people help with their personal concerns. Managers bring their private problems to work each day; problems such as marital and family difficulties, economic entanglements, physical ailments, etc. These inevitably affect their work, and many organisations both provide special psychological assistance to individuals and train their managers in counselling skills.

Providing counselling assistance to individuals has several uses. It can help the organisation to be increasingly sensitive to individual needs and concerns. Counselling can provide a bridge between organisational goals and the life situations of individuals. It helps to ensure that people are employed fully and not seriously distracted by their private problems. Giving counselling assistance can help managers to establish and maintain rapport with employees. People are treated more humanely when their bosses are counselling oriented. This part of management development can contribute to a 'family spirit'. It can help to reduce the number of people who voluntarily leave the organisation. In addition, counselling may indirectly uncover some organisational problems, such as hidden effects of inadequate compensation.

On the other hand, counselling has its difficulties. Obviously it requires special training. It can make people vulnerable. Unless it is carried out well, it can create dependency relationships. The condition of confidentiality, which is necessary in counselling, can be used manipulatively. It may undermine the effectiveness of the performance review system. It can be resented by employees. It threatens the privacy of individuals. The people who need counselling the most are often the ones who are least likely to avail themselves of the service, but the process has to be voluntary. Counselling is time-consuming, and it requires privacy that often is difficult to achieve within organisations.

Coaching

This activity has received added attention in recent years. It consists of on-the-job assistance by supervisors and/or by trainers. It is job-specific, individualised instruction. Coaching has many positive characteristics, among which are:

1   It is job relevant;
2   It requires the coach to relate to the individuals' needs and readiness;
3   It facilitates two-way communication and relationships;
4   It generates learning that is immediately applicable;
5   It is highly goal-oriented;
6   It is easily linked to performance review;
7   It requires managers (coaches) to be developmental.

One has to make the assumption in coaching that the coachee's job makes sense, but sometimes that is not the case. Coaching can also be too here-and-now oriented, training people in procedures that can become obsolete. This activity is heavily dependent upon the manager's training skills. Many managers find it easy to avoid coaching their subordinates. The activity is difficult to monitor from the outside. It may be inefficient, especially when several peoples are being individually trained in the same skills and procedures at about the same time. Like many other management development activities, coaching takes time away from normal work flow.

Organisational role analysis

This programme feature is clarifying managers' roles and functions within an organisational context. As such, it is in an ill-defined area between management development and organisation development. It consists of clarifying role expectations, preferences, and actual behaviour, and it usually includes role negotiation.

The approach provides clarity in job responsibilities and fosters a climate of negotiation. It helps to manage redundancy of role functions, and it can help to uncover system problems and can assist in the implementation of organisational changes. Organisation role analysis can help to identify deviant performers, in all directions, being easily linked with performance review.

The analysis of managerial roles can, however, be impersonal, rigid, and competitive; fostering independence rather than inter-dependence. It is time-consuming, and it frequently generates resistance, often failing to take personal feelings and aspirations into account.

Task forces/Project groups

These are United States/United Kingdom terms for essentially the same thing, creating cross-departmental groups to attack organisational problems. This practice has many benefits for developing managers. Participants learn from the cross-pollination that occurs in group deliberations. Optimal skills can be quickly applied to system concerns, while participants are gaining valuable new experience. It can promote a 'we' attitude to combat departmental insularity, thus fostering good interteam relations. It can generate thorough problem-solving processes and improve the 'fire-fighting' ability of the organisations. The work of such groups is highly 'task focused'.

Such groups may simply mirror the instability in the organisation's culture, however. Project groups can disrupt functional teams' ongoing work. If such groups are not managed effectively, they can produce unworkable solutions and non-committal outcomes. The conclusions and recommendations of these groups have to be 'sold' to decision makers. Task forces and project groups should have personal experience of teambuilding in advance to ensure their effectiveness, in order to prevent their outcomes from disrupting the system unduly.

Seminars

Seminars differ from trainings in that the 'teachers' are the students. These are teach-each-other events that are simply organised and facilitated by the training staff. They can be used for pooling the experience of managers across the organisation and to develop interpersonal support networks within the system. They can be a means for the organisation to use its learning resources well by bringing people together with common interests and/or problems. Seminars require little active participation on the part of professional trainers. They are easily scheduled and they can help to develop managers' training and communication skills and to promote the exchange of ideas.

One risk with seminars is that they can deteriorate into 'bull sessions' or 'gripe' sessions. Participants may be pooling ignorance or reinforcing each other's prejudices. Extensive use of seminars may cut out external views that might be useful for managers, and new insights may not be developed. Often seminars are not sufficiently goal-oriented to be completely effective. They may produce premature solutions to system problems, and they may falsely raise expectations.

Exchange consulting

This management development activity involves managers consulting with each other on technical and personnel problems. The advantages of this programme feature are:

1 It uses organisational abilities appropriately;
2 It brings fresh perspectives to problem situations;
3 It focuses added resources to managerial problem solving;
4 It develops consulting skills among managers;
5 It fosters a 'we' attitude;
6 It helps to break down interteam barriers;
7 It promotes interchange of personnel;
8 It aids in the career development of managers.

Managerial consulting has its liabilities, too:

1 The practice is time-consuming;
2 It requires skills that many managers do not have;
3 Ineffective consulting models, such as extensive advice-giving, may be used;

4   The activity may detract from managers' own goal attainment;
5   It can be seen as interference and/or as a threat;
6   Like counselling, it is often not asked for by those who need it
     most.

Group training programmes

This is a special type of in-house training. It is system-wide small-group-oriented training such as Managerial Grid, Coverdale, T-groups, Transactional Analysis, and Assertion Training. It is designed to create a common base of concepts and vocabulary to the entire system.

The advantages of such programmes are many and varied. Group training programmes can indeed inculcate common concepts and vocabulary into an organisation's culture. They utilise the group skills of managers, and they often require managers to stretch themselves personally. Such programmes can promote organisational 'togetherness' and can help to break down barriers. The small group activities are usually both intense and personal.

Some dangers of small-group programmes are:

1   They are threatening to a significant proportion of managers;
2   They can be inappropriately and excessively personal;
3   They can be manipulative;
4   They can damage individuals;
5   They can promote dysfunctional organisational norms;
6   They require specialised skills on the part of the trainers;
7   They are often 'faddy' or 'trendy';
8   They can come to resemble religion.

THE MANAGEMENT DEVELOPMENT ACTIVITY ASSESSMENT

The seventeen programme activities discussed above have been cast into instrument form in the Management Development Activity Assessment (MDAA). This questionnaire can be used to evaluate the various components of an organisation's programme for developing managers. Items in the instrument parallel the discussion immediately above. Each item contains a brief summary of the discussion and a rating scale.

The MDAA can be used in several ways. Most obviously, it can form the basis of a training department self study. Each member of the staff fills out the instrument independently, without prior discussion of the elements of the management development programme. When all have completed the scale, their data are pooled on the summary page. Then the staff study the distributions of ratings to isolate those programme aspects that need to be strengthened and added. Of course, this process can also be carried out singly by the training manager, but involving others in the process possibly increases ownership of the programme.

If the management development programme has a 'steering committee' of managers, these people can fill out the MDAA also, in order to generate a prioritised agenda for improvement. We believe strongly that the programme should receive the oversight of managers in order to correlate management development with organisational policy. Even if there is no group outside the training department that is responsible for directing the major directions that trainers take, it is good practice to find ways of obtaining management input for planning. Accordingly, the MDAA can be used in a survey of a sample of managers to determine their views of the programme.

Items can be added to the MDAA to make it more useful to the organisation. It is probably best to maintain the item format of the instrument in order to generate paralleled data. Programme features not covered by the questionnaire are described by a group of people who can be honest about both the advantages and the potential disadvantages of each feature. The summary format at the end contains space for data from three organisation-unique items.

Instructions

Below are listed seventeen activities that are often included in management development programmes. Each is briefly defined, and the advantages and disadvantages of each are listed. Evaluate each activity according to how it relates to your management development programme. Place a check mark (✓) in the appropriate place on the rating scale included in each item. Do not leave any items blank.

1   *In-house training* Courses organised by trainers and conducted internally.

Advantages	*Disadvantages*
In-company knowledge and skills	May become in-bred
Establishes/maintains organisational culture, norms, formal practices	May not be company specific
Useful with dispersed units	

A   A strong feature of our programme   ☐
B   A moderately successful feature   ☐
C   An area needing improvement   ☐
D   An option not available but which should be   ☐
E   Not applicable to our organisation   ☐

2   *External training* Sending persons to outside courses, for special training and/or academic degrees.

Advantages	*Disadvantages*
Increased sensitivity to events in external environment	May not be relevant to the organisational needs
Develops emotional resilience	Expensive
Cross-cultural impact	Fashionable
Bridges gaps between organisations	Seen as holiday or 'perk'
New ideas and approaches	Difficult to apply back home
Challenges assumptions	Can create barriers back home

A A strong feature of our programme ☐
B A moderately successful feature ☐
C An area needing improvement ☐
D An option not available but which should be ☐
E Not applicable to our organisation ☐

3 *Training centre* An organisation-oriented training facility usually restricted to in-house training.

Advantages	*Disadvantages*
Facilitates development of in-house training	Must be used often
	May become an empire
Maximum control of venue/ schedule	May become an ivory tower
	May become an organisational burden
Highlights training in the organisation	Requires management
	Keeps trainers isolated
Potentially holds expense down	May add travel expense
Clearinghouse for ideas	

A A strong feature of our programme ☐
B A moderately successful feature ☐
C An area needing much improvement ☐
D Not available but should be ☐
E Not applicable to our organisation ☐

4 *Performance review* Regularly scheduled appraisals of employee job performance.

Advantages	*Disadvantages*
Provides for individual goal setting	May not be carried out honestly
Better manager-subordinate communication	Bureaucratic
	Time-consuming
Improved interpersonal relationships	May be perfunctory
	Sometimes not goal-oriented
Promotes better career planning/guidance	Confused with salary review
Helps to develop employees	

A A strong feature of our programme ☐
B A moderately successful feature ☐
C An area needing improvement ☐
D An option not available but which should be ☐
E Not applicable to our organisation ☐

5   *Career development* Counselling service for employees to manage their own careers within the organisation.

Advantages	*Disadvantages*
Helps people to manage themselves	May raise false expectations
Provides data for overall management development	Opportunities may be insufficient
Provides data for individual choices	Can lead to dissatisfaction and seeking alternative employment
Facilitates proper employment of people	Too much focus on the individual, not enough on organisational demands
Pressurises managers to be developmental	

A   A strong feature of our programme   ☐
B   A moderately successful feature   ☐
C   An area needing improvement   ☐
D   An option not available but which should be   ☐
E   Not applicable to our organisation   ☐

6   *Job rotation* Programmatic shifting through various jobs to develop skills, technical expertise, and perspective.

Advantages	*Disadvantages*
Gives wide experience	Requires frequent job adjustments
Generates perspective/ 'worldwiseness'	Interferes with ongoing processes
New ideas, skills, expertise	May result in coping rather than learning
Challenges accepted order	May not generate 'helicopter' perspective
Cross-fertilisation	Seen as a threat

A   A strong feature of our programme   ☐
B   A moderately successful feature   ☐
C   An area needing improvement   ☐
D   An option not available but which should be   ☐
E   Not applicable to our organisation   ☐

7   *Secondments* Temporary assignments, usually within other organisations.

Advantages	Disadvantages
Cross-pollination	Resistance
Influx of skills to area where needed	Entry/re-entry problems
	Administrative nuisance
Rapid problem solving in host organisation	Inappropriate assignments
	Thankless
Development of 'helicopter' view	

A   A strong feature of our programme ☐
B   A moderately successful feature ☐
C   An area needing improvement ☐
D   An option not available but which should be ☐
E   Not applicable to our organisation ☐

8   *International assignments* Temporary assignments within organisations in other countries.

Advantages	Disadvantages
Cross-pollination	Language/cultural difficulties
Influx of skills to area where needed	Expense
	Learning not directly applicable back home
Rapid problem solving in host organisation	Entry/re-entry problems
Development of 'helicopter' understanding	Administrative nuisance
	Inappropriate assignments
Promotes international understanding	Thankless
	May be seen as vacation/'perk'
May make useful contacts	

A   A strong feature of our programme ☐
B   A moderately successful feature ☐
C   An area needing improvement ☐
D   An option not available but which should be ☐
E   Not applicable to our organisation ☐

9   *Using consultants* Bringing in outside trainers to work in management development activities.

Advantages	*Disadvantages*
Expands resources available for development	May be insensitive to organisational nuances
New ideas, fresh approach	Expensive
Challenges current practices	No ongoing responsibility
No vested interest	May circumvent internal trainers
May help train internal trainers	May foster dependency
Minimum disruption of managers	'Solution in search of a problem'
Flexibly scheduled	May be primarily entertainers

A   A strong feature of our programme   ☐
B   A moderately successful feature   ☐
C   An area needing improvement   ☐
D   An option not available but which should be   ☐
E   Not applicable to our organisation   ☐

10   *Mentoring* Assigning more senior managers to assist new managers in growing into their jobs.

Advantages	*Disadvantages*
Involves senior management in management development	Takes valuable senior management time
Provides practical guidance	May generate insubordination
May ignore performance review	May promote jealousy, 'favoured person' image
Improves 'up-down communication'	
Provides 'godfather' assistance	
Gives ombudsman potential	

A   A strong feature of our programme   ☐
B   A moderately successful feature   ☐
C   An area needing improvement   ☐
D   An option not available but which should be   ☐
E   Not applicable to our organisation   ☐

11 *Counselling* Personal development help for employees in their private concerns.

Advantages	Disadvantages
Sensitive to individual needs	Requires special training
Promotes appropriate employment	May make people vulnerable
	Can create dependency
Bridges personal-organisational goals	Creates condition of confidentiality
Maintains rapport with employees	May undermine performance review
Treats people humanely	Can be resented
Fosters family spirit	Threatens privacy
Reduces people seeking other employment	Often not asked for even when needed
May uncover organisational problems	Time-consuming
	Requires privacy

A A strong feature of our programme ☐
B A moderately successful feature ☐
C An area needing improvement ☐
D An option not available but which should be ☐
E Not applicable to our organisation ☐

12 *Coaching* On-the-job assistance by supervisors and/or by trainers.

Advantages	Disadvantages
Job relevant	Assumes the job makes sense
Related to individual needs	May be too 'here-and-now'
Facilitates up-down communication and relationships	Dependent on manager's training skills
	Easy to avoid
Immediately applicable learning	Difficult to monitor
Goal-oriented	May be inefficient
Easily linked to performance review	Interrupts work flow
Makes managers developmental	
Involves managers in development	

A   A strong feature of our programme   ☐
B   A moderately successful feature   ☐
C   An area needing improvement   ☐
D   An option not available but which should be ☐
E   Not applicable to our organisation   ☐

13 *Organisational role analysis* Clarifying managers' roles within
the organisational context.

Advantages	*Disadvantages*
Provides clarity in responsibilities	Can be impersonal, rigid, competitive
Fosters negotiation	Can foster independence rather than interdependence
Helps manage redundancy of functions	May fail to take personal feelings and aspirations into account
Can uncover system problems	Time-consuming
Helps implement organisational change	Generates resistance
Identifies deviant performers	
Easily linked to performance review	

A   A strong feature of our programme   ☐
B   A moderately successful feature   ☐
C   An area needing improvement   ☐
D   An option not available but which should be ☐
E   Not applicable to our organisation   ☐

14 *Task forces/Project groups* Cross-departmental groups that study
organisational problems, and/or carry out special assignments.

Advantages	*Disadvantages*
Cross-pollination	May mirror organisational instability
Optional skills applied	Can disrupt functional work teams
New experience	Can produce unworkable solutions
Promotes 'we' attitude	May generate non-committal outcomes
Fosters interteam relations	Outcomes must be 'sold'
Thorough problem solving	Requires advance experience of teambuilding
Improves organisation's fire-fighting ability	Can disrupt the system
Highly task focused	

A   A strong feature of our programme ☐
B   A moderately successful feature ☐
C   An area needing improvement ☐
D   An option not available but which should be ☐
E   Not applicable to our organisation ☐

15   *Seminars* Teach-each-other events for pooling experience.

Advantages	*Disadvantages*
Pools experience	May turn into 'bull'/'gripe'
Develops interpersonal	sessions
support	May pool ignorance,
Uses resources well	reinforce prejudice
Flexibly scheduled	Can cut out external view
Develops managers' training	Does not bring in new insight
and communication skills	Often not goal-oriented
Exchange of ideas	May generate premature
	solutions
	Can falsely raise expectations

A   A strong feature of our programme ☐
B   A moderately successful feature ☐
C   An area needing improvement ☐
D   An option not available but which should be ☐
E   Not applicable to our organisation ☐

16   *Exchange consulting* Managers consulting with each other on technical and/or personnel problems.

Advantages	*Disadvantages*
Uses organisational abilities	Time-consuming
appropriately	Requires special skills
Brings fresh perspective	May be too advice-oriented
Gives added resources	Can detract from manager's
Develops consulting skills	own goals
Fosters 'we' attitude	Can be seen as interference
Breaks down barriers	Threatening
Promotes interchange of	Often not asked for, even
personnel	when needed
Aids career development	

A   A strong feature of our programme   □
B   A moderately successful feature   □
C   An area needing improvement   □
D   An option not available but which should be   □
E   Not applicable to our organisation   □

17 *Group training programmes* System wide, small-group-oriented training, such as Managerial Grid, Coverdale, T-groups, Transactional Analysis, Assertion Training.

Advantages	*Disadvantages*
Common concepts/language	Threatening
Utilises group skills	Can be too personal
Seen as real	Can be manipulative
Stretches managers personally	May damage individuals
Promotes 'togetherness'	Can promote dysfunctional
Intensive	norms
Personal	Requires special skills
	May be 'faddy' or 'trendy'
	Can resemble religion

A   A strong feature of our programme   □
B   A moderately successful feature   □
C   An area needing improvement   □
D   An option not available but should be   □
E   Not applicable to our organisation   □

PROGRAMME

If more than one person has completed this assessment, summarise the ratings in the form below to develop an action planning agenda to improve the programme. If you conducted this assessment alone, transfer your item ratings to the grid below for overall study.

Management development activity	A. A strong feature of your programme	B. A moderately successful feature	C. An area needing improvement	D. An option not available but which should be	E. Not applicable here
1 In-house training					
2 External training					
3 Training centre					
4 Performance review					
5 Career development					
6 Job rotation					
7 Secondments					
8 International assignments					
9 Using consultants					
10 Mentoring					
11 Counselling					
12 Coaching					
13 Organisational role analysis					
14 Task forces/project groups					
15 Seminars					
16 Exchange consulting					
17 Group training programmes					

OVERALL PROGRAMME EFFECTIVENESS

We have looked at the self-assessed effectiveness of major management development activities. Now we turn our attention to organisational conditions and practices that can determine the overall effectiveness of the programme. It is possible to have well-designed programme elements and still not meet the needs of the organisation for developing its managers. Research and authoritative opinion are available to shed light on how the organisation should support its management development programme and how trainers should focus their work on organisational goals.

The second instrument of this introductory chapter, the Management Development Audit (MDA) is based on a mixture of the findings of 'objective' research studies conducted both in the United States and the United Kingdom and on the judgements of management development observers. The bibliographic references are built into the instrument, for the guidance of those who wish to read the detailed background.

Like the MDAA, the MDA can be used in several ways. Its most immediate relevance is to the training staff, but it can also be filled in by the supervisors of the programme and by a sample of managers. Items can be added to the MDA so long as they can be validly scored along on a five-point scale of effectiveness. Of course, the MDA can be used in conjunction with the MDAA to provide a more comprehensive view of the adequacy of the programme and its support.

The order of the items in the MDA has been randomised, and eighteen are worded 'negatively', that is, their scoring is reversed. These two development techniques were used to minimise response biases, but they complicate the scoring and interpretation. The best use of the MDA is to develop an agenda for group discussion (problem identification, problem solving) of individual items isolated by the scoring procedure. Guidelines to assist in this process are built into the scoring and interpretation sheet that follows the MDA.

MANAGEMENT DEVELOPMENT AUDIT

Introduction

Read each of the following items, think how descriptive it is of the situation in your organisation, and indicate its appropriateness by using the following scale:

SA *Strongly agree* that this is the situation in our organisation.

A *Agree* that this condition exists.

U *Undecided* or *uncertain* that this describes our situation.

D *Disagree* that this statement is true here.

SD *Strongly disagree* that this is true in our organisation.

_____ 1 Substantial resources are committed to ensure the completeness and continuity of the management development programme in our organisation.

_____ 2 Basically, the management development manager is the person responsible for the development of managers.

_____ 3 The strengths and weaknesses of the management development programme are systematically analysed here.

_____ 4 In this organisation specific job assignments are made to utilise new skills after managerial development occurs.

_____ 5 Policies that guide management development are published widely within our organisation.

_____ 6 The organisation recognises that management development is the task of line management.

_____ 7 In planning organisational changes, we take managerial capability into account.

_____ 8 There is no formal appraisal system here.

_____ 9 Participation in university programmes is primarily at the top management level.

_____ 10 Management development here is viewed as apart from, but complemented by, analytical technique and functional training.

_____ 11 Our organisation operates a training establishment or centre.

_____ 12 The organisation emphasises managerial self-development through activities designed to meet both the organisation's and the individual's needs.

_____ 13 Management training is seen here as both a service function, ensuring that basic standards are maintained, *and* as a way of continually developing the organisation.

_____ 14 Formal training in the management skills required at different job levels is used to prepare for and enhance on-the-job development.

_____ 15 The ability of the manager to develop people is a significant element in his or her performance evaluation.

_____ 16 The organisation sends people to outside institutions for development.

_____ 17 The training programme emphasises the management of people.

_____ 18 People in positions of power and influence here seem to be largely ignorant of the link between organisational and individual goals.

_____ 19 Management development policy is set up by the board of directors.

_____ 20 Our organisation stresses that it is the responsibility of individual managers to improve their own performance, assisted and encouraged by the organisation's programmes.

_____ 21 Performance reviews here are carried out for a variety of purposes.

_____ 22 The training curriculum concentrates on technical/ operational areas of knowledge.

_____ 23 The management development programme has been designed to be unique to this organisation.

_____ 24 Training activities in this organisation are directly and logically derived from overall organisational objectives.

_____ 25 There is little or no adaption of the management development programme to the organisation's aims.

_____ 26 The chief executive officer supports the management development programme.

_____ 27 Performance appraisals here focus only on salary administration.

_____ 28 Management development activities are given significant attention by top management personnel.

_____ 29 Training here is geared to business plans.

_____ 30 The organisation operates its management development 'behind closed doors'.

_____ 31 Around here training is done as an 'act of faith'.

_____ 32 Bosses in this organisation have the ability to provide
the appropriate conditions for development to occur.

_____ 33 Training is limited to what the organisation's internal
capabilities will permit.

_____ 34 Management development is clearly linked with
corporate plans.

_____ 35 Identifying personnel for management development is
based on an assessment of the individual's potential as
a manager.

_____ 36 There is no coherent policy for management development in this organisation.

_____ 37 Development of subordinates, including coaching and
career planning, is a definite responsibility of all
managers.

_____ 38 In this organisation trainers decide on what is to be
done in management development.

_____ 39 The organisation provides coaching to develop its
managers.

_____ 40 There is a common philosophy that development
occurs on-the-job.

_____ 41 Appraisals here focus only on the last year's work.

_____ 42 Job rotation is a definite aspect of the management
development programme in this organisation.

_____ 43 In this organisation management development
managers are not involved in the corporate planning
process.

_____ 44 The management development programme in our
organisation features in-house training, supplemented
by lectures from guests, consultants and faculty
members.

_____ 45 The management development policy here covers a
small, élite group of employees.

_____ 46 The organisation engages in meaningful succession
planning.

_____ 47 Individuals in this organisation are given no voice in
their development.

_____ 48 Employees are encouraged to discuss their appraisals
with their managers in forward-looking interviews.

_____ 49   The policy that governs management development here is formed by the head of the training department.

_____ 50   In our organisation the management development policy covers a high proportion of employees.

_____ 51   The management development programme focuses on improving the effectiveness of those managers directly involved in the main business of the organisation and those tackling the main problems of its continuance.

_____ 52   This organisation emphasises development toward both organisational and individual goals.

_____ 53   There is no training centre operated by our organisation.

_____ 54   Managers in this organisation are primarily developed on-the-job.

_____ 55   Appraisals attempt to identify the development need of the individuals, including his or her view, translated into meaningful objectives.

_____ 56   Management development is viewed here more as a system than an on-the-job activity.

_____ 57   In this organisation self-development activities are viewed as an indication of a person's commitment to make a contribution and to develop his or her skills to the fullest.

_____ 58   Managerial potential is identified by the use of assessment centres.

_____ 59   Management development here begins before or during the person's first management job.

_____ 60   No succession plans are developed in this organisation.

MDA SCORING AND INTERPRETATION WORKSHEET

Instructions

Most MDA items are worded in such a way that agreement with them gives more points than disagreement. There are eighteen items on which the scoring is reversed. Follow this simple procedure for scoring the MDA.

1   Circle the *item numbers* of the following items:

2, 8, 18, 22, 25, 27, 30, 31, 33, 36, 38, 41, 43, 45, 47, 49, 53 and 60.

2   In front of these items assign the following scores:
SA = 1, A = 2, U = 3, D = 4, SD = 5.

3   Now go back and score all the remaining items in the *reverse* way:
SA = 5, A = 4, U = 3, D = 2, SD = 1.

4   Add up all of the sixty item scores to obtain the overall score, and write it in the box provided. This score can range from 60 to 300.

OVERALL SCORE

The higher the score the closer the management development programme is to 'ideal' situations, according to research and authoritative opinion. A rough idea of what the score means is given in the following scale:

252–300   Conditions are extremely favourable for the organisation's management development programme to be successful.

204–251   The organisation's management development is being supported adequately, but there is room for growth.

156–203   If the management development programme is to meet the needs of both the system and its employees, it clearly needs more management support.

108–155   There are numerous conditions in this organisation that make it difficult for the management development programme to be effective.

60–107   It is unlikely that management development can be carried out well under these organisational conditions.

If several persons completed the MDA, tally their scores in the boxes below. Look for 'bunching' of scores to determine overall programme assessment.

☐	280–300
☐	260–279
☐	240–259
☐	220–239
☐	200–219
☐	180–199
☐	160–179
☐	140–159
☐	120–139
☐	100–119
☐	80–99
☐	60–79

To develop an 'agenda' of action items in order to improve these conditions, look at the actual items of the MDA. Find those items that scored 1 and 2 (or 4 and 5 in the 'negative' items). Generate lists of each for staff discussion, problem identification, and problem solving. Items which scored 1 could be labelled 'support deficiencies', and those that scored 2 could be termed 'support weaknesses'. Data sheets such as the following can be useful in guiding group discussion.

Management development support deficiencies
MDA Data

Item number	Number scoring '1' (or '5' in negative)	Item topic

Management development support weaknesses
MDA Data

Item number	Number scoring '2' (or '4' in negative)	Item topic

NOTES AND REFERENCES

*Atwood, L. T., 'Management Development in British companies', *Journal of European Industrial Training,* vol. 3, no. 8, 1979, pp. 1–32.

*Denning, R. W., Hussey, D. E., and Newman, P. G., *Management Development: What to Look For.* London: Harbridge House Europe, 1978.

*Digman, L. A., 'How well-managed organizations develop their executives', *Organizational Dynamics,* Autumn, 1978, pp. 63–80.

Foy, N., 'Management education: Current action and future needs', *Journal of European Industrial Training,* 1979, vol. 3, no. 2, pp. 1–28.

Management Training and Development, Part 1. London: Food, Drink and Tobacco Industry Training Board (No date).

*Newman, P.G., 'Development: For and against'. *Management Today,* August, 1978, pp. 31–32.

Peter, L. J. and Hull, R., *The Peter Principle.* New York: Morrow, 1969.

Pfeiffer, J. W., 'The "cascade" model of performance appraisal', *Group and Organization Studies,* September, 1979, *4,* 3, 316–321.

Pfeiffer, J. W., 'The "cascade" model of performance appraisal', *Group and Organizational Studies,* September, 1979, vol. 4, no. 3, pp. 316–321.

Pfeiffer, J. W., and Jones, J. E., 'OD readiness', in Pfeiffer, J. W. and Jones, J. E. (eds) *The Annual Handbook for Group Facilitators,* San Diego, California: University Associates, 1978.

For those management development staffs that wish to study the research and opinion underlying the MDA in more detail, the references marked with an asterisk will be helpful.

2 Managerial competence

In recent years managers have had to face new and more intense problems in directing the work of their subordinates. Labour difficulties, energy shortages, rising costs, lack of capital, and increased government regulations have all contributed to problems of productivity and profitability. The manager has to work under pressure to achieve organisational goals in spite of the complications of modern economics. Small countries control the flow of large amounts of capital. New laws governing how one hires and fires people have been passed. People no longer seem committed to working fairly for a fair wage. Soaring interest rates have made improvement of plant and machinery difficult. Public-pressure groups attempt to force organisations to change their products and services, conserve the environment, and alter their consumption of energy. The marketplace has become less predictable. When our fathers entered the workforce, managers had a great deal of power and were able to follow their own judgement. They could be authoritarian, arbitrary, vindictive and parental. They could fire a worker for little or no cause. Since then the rules have changed, and the changes are irreversible. People now know how to organise against managers, and they have legal supports that they can use in the process. Managers must now be careful not to foul the environment, waste energy, or discriminate against women and minority groups. All of these changes that affect the work of managers require that they look at their responsibilities differently. Also, it is more imperative than ever to keep in touch with changes in the outside world. The individual manager has to accomplish tasks by supervising the work of others in a world which contains more pressures and restrictions than ever before.

All of these changes put pressure on management development specialists to make their programmes keep pace with what managers need to learn. In order to maximise the effectiveness of management development programmes, professionals need an organised way of conceptualising managerial competencies. It is difficult to imagine that programme planning can be effected in an orderly way without isolating the desired learning and changes in managerial behaviour. Model-based analysis and development is preferable to *ad hoc* course additions ('We need a training session on stress here') because it offers comprehensiveness, integration, and the long-range view. It is not enough to provide good courses for managers. The management development staff must determine what managerial behaviours can be changed to improve productivity. Essentially, management development represents changes in managerial behaviour, and specialists charged with promoting these changes need to be sensitive to how managers relate to change.

In this chapter we show how the 'motivation problem' that managers often complain about can be largely under their conscious control. Part of what enervates managers is their attitudes toward change, and we demonstrate how working *with* changes is more productive than resisting it. Since there has been confusion in the past regarding common terminology in management development, we define our terms before proceeding, to lay out our competency model, step by step.

MOTIVATION

The work of the manager is primarily directed towards other people rather than towards things. It is because of this that we believe that managers can increase their effectiveness in facing current problems. The manager can do little about world economics, the larger culture that shapes people's values, or the cost of resources needed to attain organisational goals. These are already established; but there are many things that are under the managers' control, and these things can lead to greater productivity and satisfaction. Managers often ask, 'How do I motivate my people?' Of course, there is no simple answer to that question. Then what can help managers guide the work of their subordinates in a rapidly changing world? We believe that managing in accord with the following principles points the way towards improving the 'lack of motivation' among subordinates:

1 People behave the way they do at work for two reasons: the kind of people they are (personality) and how they are treated (management and human relations).

2 It is exceedingly difficult to change the basic personalities of people, but their behaviour will change directly if managers treat them differently.

3 The manager has a wide range of possibilities in how to treat people. These options go all the way from absolute control to non-directive support.

4 Managers can influence how workers behave in relation to each other. Meetings and mediations are routine aspects of being a manager.

5 Relationships between the manager and workers and within the worker group can have powerful effects on people's behaviour. Group norms can either hamper productivity ('Nobody hurries around here') or support growth and development.

6 Workers perform in ways that they believe will give them satisfying rewards. They simply predict the outcomes of and rewards for their behaviour.

7 What is rewarding for one person may not be seen as desirable by another. One may seek management approval while others seek more money, position, influence, or interesting work.

8 The manager needs to be aware of what motivates each individual subordinate and treat each accordingly.

9 The manager has to devise a flexible system of rewarding workers both formally (pay and perks) and informally (recognition, ego-boosts, etc.).

10 Motivating employees means communicating and negotiating with them both as individuals and as a group.

The manager does have considerable leeway, then, in affecting the behaviour of employees even if there are many things constantly changing that are out of his or her control. The most important principles that managers should apply are to know themselves, improve people skills, talk *with* instead of *to* subordinates, avoid stereotyping them, and be sensitive to what they want out of their work. From the individual manager's perspective the most promising strategy in attacking productivity problems is to concentrate on how to influence the behaviour of workers. That means separating what can be changed from what cannot. The manager can change his or her self image, develop more skills in working with people, learn how to work with groups more effectively, alter how the work unit relates to other parts of the organisation, and improve relations with customers, clients and suppliers on the outside.

THE MANAGER AND CHANGE

How does the individual manager relate to changes outside his or her area of responsibility? Some welcome change, and others resist it. Consider a meeting that is called to announce and explain policy changes in the organisation. Often during such meetings managers ask questions, but they withhold their reactions. As soon as the meeting is over, they go outside with their friends and complain about the changes. This is sometimes called the 'parking-lot phenomenon'.

The meeting outside is often more powerful in shaping the manager's behaviour than the formal one. Some managers attend the meeting inside with a different set of attitudes. They are looking for opportunities and solutions to problems facing their units. They may propose policy changes or interpretations favourable to themselves.

One way of thinking about how managers respond to organisational changes is to list the most common patterns along a line that extends from counterproductive to productive. Some ways managers respond are not in the best interests of either themselves or the organisation. Other managerial behaviours get the job done.

Counterproductive – *Sabotage.* Undermining changes through covert activity.
 – *Overt resistance.* Openly attempting to reverse changes.
 – *Passive resistance.* Withholding support for changes.
 – *Denial.* Failing to acknowledge the reality of changes.
 – *Avoidance.* Adopting a low profile regarding changes.
 – *Blaming.* Making changes the fault of other persons.

- *Moaning and groaning.* Complaining about changes.
- *Confronting.* Challenging the rationality and probable effects of changes.
- *Problem solving.* Dealing with the effects of changes.
- *Planning.* Anticipating changes and the need for changes in the future.

Productive
- *Making changes happen.* Introducing needed changes.

Towards the counterproductive end of the list we are referring to managers who tend to work *against* change. At the productive end managers are working *with* change. In between lie most managers, who are annoyed by the fact that the work situation never seems to stay the same for long.

It is our view that it takes just about the same amount of human energy to attempt to restrain change as it does to accept its inevitability and work inside it productively. Put another way, it is just as easy to make yourself happy as it is to make yourself miserable. It is simply energy that is transformed by the attitudes of the manager. Is the glass half empty or half full? If managers look optimistically at the behaviour of their subordinates and at the changes that their organisations experience, they are likely to be able to find ways of managing themselves and their employees effectively. The attitude that 'nothing can be done' saps energy. The approach that asks 'What are my options?' often increases the ability to make productive decisions regarding change.

SOME TERMINOLOGY

We use many titles for managers. In the United States and in the United Kingdom we frequently hear such terms as chief executive officer, executive, senior manager, managing director, middle manager, line manager, staff manager, first-line supervisor, foreman and overseer. What do these people have in common? Each is in an official position of authority over other persons. Each attempts to influence the behaviour of others in order to attain organisational goals. Each is accountable for the productivity of a unit of the organisation. When we begin to consider whether persons with these titles are carrying out their responsibilities effectively, we need to define some of our terms. Since it is the purpose of this book to help management developers to help managers behave more effectively, let us look at some key ideas.

Management

This is a term that means getting work done through the efforts of others. Traditionally, it means planning the work flow (queuing up tasks), directing the task behaviour of subordinates, controlling the quality of employee's behaviour and evaluating the outcomes of their production. Of course, managers do many things in addition to managing others' work, such as engaging in public relations and negotiating with other departments.

Supervision

This term refers to controlling the behaviour of subordinates according to a set of standards for their behaviour. Seen this way, supervision is one aspect of managing. In general executives set policy and goals, managers establish strategy for their implementation, and supervisors see to it that the policy and goals are realised by workers.

Leadership

This is the same as influence. You are leading when you are persuasive, when people submit to your guidance. This may occur informally, for example in choosing a restaurant for dinner. It represents the use of power, as opposed to 'pulling rank' by the exercise of authority.

In our view then, managers engage in both supervision and leadership behaviours, in addition to playing a number of other roles within the organisation. They pass on information, make decisions, solve problems, set goals, intervene in conflict, run meetings, appraise the performance of their subordinates, make deals with other managers, and carry out ceremonies.

Efficiency and effectiveness

We find it useful to make a distinction between efficiency and effectiveness since confusing these ideas can lead to inefficiency and ineffectiveness.

Efficiency. This usually means getting the most output for the least input. A system, process or behaviour is considered efficient when it (a) works reliably, (b) produces desired results, and (c) requires minimal energy. Trying to find the best ways of doing things is the search for efficiency.

Effectiveness. This idea goes beyond efficiency. We are now concerned with both short term and long term effects. We use the term to mean accomplishing goals that are consistent with both the immediate and long-range requirements of the system.

The effective manager is seen as one who has a positive concept of self, who has a well-thought-out position regarding how to manage others, who takes care of himself or herself, who has clear personal values, whose manner of influencing others is adaptable, who is organisation-oriented, and who has highly developed skills. These skills include communication, goal setting, problem solving, decision making, managing conflict, generating teamwork, conducting meetings, evaluating the performance of subordinates, coaching individual employees, counselling, negotiating, planning, relating to the public, interviewing and training. By contrast the ineffective manager has a negative self view, has no consistent rationale for how to manage others' work, neglects personal health, has ill defined personal values, is rigid in his or her management style, manages with little or no regard for organisational priorities, and lacks many of the core skills just listed. Looked at in this way, effectiveness in managerial behaviour means being well in control of the situation, and ineffectiveness means struggling to cope.

A MODEL OF MANAGERIAL COMPETENCIES

The manager's job requires the playing of many roles. Mintzberg (1975) outlined ten:

Figurehead	
Leader	Interpersonal
Liaison	
Monitor	
Disseminator	Informal
Spokesman	
Entrepreneur	
Disturbance handler	Decisional
Resource allocator	
Negotiator	

The competencies needed to carry out all of these responsibilities are many, and comprehensive management development programmes should address them thoroughly. It is not enough to think of the manager's job as planning, organising, co-ordinating and controlling – the classic view. Managers have to function in increasingly open systems and have to be effective while 'wearing many different hats'. While meeting all of these challenges, the manager has to manage his or her own growth towards personal effectiveness as well.

What distinguishes effective from ineffective, or less effective, managers? The question is significant to anyone who has responsibility for developing managerial talent within an organisation. We felt that it was important to provide an organised answer, and our competencies model was developed as a response. We wanted to systemise what we believed to be important in making certain that programme development could be ensured to be comprehensive. The advantages of model-building are chiefly that:

1   The process is heuristic, that is, it leads to new knowledge or more effective inquiry;
2   It organises what is known according to a logical scheme or a psychological one;
3   It guides behaviour beyond the actual development of the model;
4   It reduces complexity to a system about which decisions can be made;
5   It is iterative in that the process itself is dynamic and the result is always open to refinement;
6   It helps us to judge what is important. So the process we went through in creating the model to be explicated here was instructive to us and has led to a construction that we believe to be useful in guiding management development programmes. We were looking for 'holism', or comprehensiveness that includes the Gestalt, or a sense of integration. It was not enough to have a morphology of necessary managerial competencies. There needed to be a kind of glue that would bind the elements together.

In searching for a way to explain what we mean by effective managerial behaviour we challenged each other's beliefs, attitudes, values, assumptions, and prejudices. We explored our own experiences as managers, consultants, and management development trainers. We reflected on what we had learned in working with thousands of managers in the past and on what other 'experts' had said about the subject of effectiveness. We wanted not only to isolate those individual characteristics that would distinguish between effective and ineffective managers but also to look at an overall view of effectiveness – a holistic picture that would at once show the parts and their relation to each other. We began with some position statements.

Self management sets a ceiling on managerial effectiveness. Managers who look after themselves have more energy available for directing the work of others. On the other hand, managers who feel stressed, who do not direct their own career development and create situations for their own advancement waste a lot of time and energy that might otherwise be available for organisational tasks.

Awareness of self leads to more effective choices. If your values and goals are clear, and you are conscious of your own reasons for managing the way you do, you are likely to accomplish your objectives both more easily and effectively. If, however, you are not in touch with your inner life (feelings, attitudes, beliefs, values, etc.) you may be driven by forces that you do not understand. You may make 'good' decisions intuitively, but we believe that managers who take into account both their hunches and the results of analytical thinking are most likely to behave effectively.

Managing implies choosing, and the key to effective management is effective choosing. The manager who is good at decision making will probably be more effective than the one who procrastinates, operates unsystematically, and does not reflect on the process of decision making.

Managing human resources is different from managing other resources. People are conscious of how they are being treated and react accordingly. As a consequence the manager has to become skilful in predicting the probability of their acceptance of his or her choices. Effective managers take the needs and feelings of others into account in decision making.

Being proactive is better than being reactive. 'Proactive' means making things happen in order to achieve your aims. 'Reactive' means waiting for things to happen and then responding. We believe strongly that effective management means *initiating* changes that are needed for the accomplishment of organisational goals.

The manager's behaviour has a systemic effect. To quote the English poet, John Donne, 'No man is an island, entire of itself'. Effective managers are sensitive to the 'ripple effects' of their choices on other organisational units.

Managers are interdependent. Although many seem not to recognise it or behave accordingly, managers need each other in order to attain organisational success. Ineffective managers often behave autonomously, building empires instead of looking for ways to co-operate. Effective managers accept the fact of interdependence and manage their relations with other organisational units in a problem-solving way.

Effective management means crossing boundaries. The formal and informal structures of the organisation are established to achieve system aims. Effective managers look for ways to penetrate counter-productive structures and to find ways through the system to make the work of their subordinates better. Ineffective managers tend to succumb to the weight of the system. They catch the diseases of the organisation.

Precedent can choke managers. Some managers seem intimidated by the history of the organisation. They take the easy road, opting to support 'the way things have always been done around here'. Effective managers see all organisational situations as unique, and they look for creative ways of overcoming barriers to goal attainment.

Systematic analysis leads to better implementation. In layman's terms, we have the 'principle of five p's': poor planning precedes puny performance. Effective managers anticipate the need for planning and prepare for changes in work situations in a step-by-step way. This does not mean that the entire process deals only with facts. Feelings and intuition are often invaluable data for planning. If contingencies are covered, including how employees are likely to feel, implementation of plans is probably going to be more effective.

Model-based behaviour is likely to be more effective. Managers who have organised rationales for their behaviours usually make better choices. Ineffective managers seem to be 'following their noses' and are inarticulate about their theories and methods. Effective managers know that nothing succeeds better than good theory.

Explicit models are better than implicit ones. Every manager has within himself or herself numerous models that have been accumulated through experience. We feel strongly that managers can increase their effectiveness by raising their consciousness about their beliefs and assumptions and by comparing these with others.

Managerial effectiveness requires continuous development. Effectiveness is a journey, not a station. Managers need to commit themselves to a career-long process of personal and professional growth in order to ensure their continued effectiveness. You never arrive, but, as the French say, you exist in a state of arrival: 'J'arrive'.

Effective human resource management implies two-way interaction. Effective managers understand that there must be both give and take, that communication must flow both ways, and that his or her continued development requires data about the effects of managerial behaviour and about people's needs.

The essential dimension of effectiveness is reflection. The core personal growth processes are self-assessment, self disclosure, feedback, risk-taking, and 'consensual validation'. In other words, you must continually look at yourself, show yourself to others, find out about the effects of your behaviour on others, try new ways of behaving, and check the perceptions others have of you through more than one source. Managing your own learning, then, means communicating honestly with others about yourself. Ineffective managers often 'keep them guessing', sometimes deliberately. Effective managers realise that they are transparent and that it takes less energy to be open than to withhold.

THE GENERAL MODEL

Since it is our belief that effectiveness is centred around the ability of the manager to take care of his or herself, we selected a concentric circle model that has as its core the individual manager. Around this centre we placed the management of subordinates, managing relationships between the manager's department and others in the organisation, and finally relations with other people outside the immediate organisation. The general picture is shown in Figure 2.1.

These four 'levels' of responsibility that each manager has require different knowledge and skills. It is obvious from the diagram that our concept of managerial effectiveness concentrates on the individual manager.

MANAGING SELF

The centre ring takes in all of those characteristics and skills that we believe constitute the core of managerial effectiveness, i.e. managing

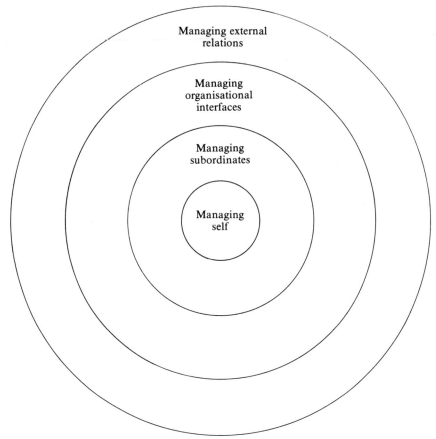

Figure 2.1

self. We believe that a manager who is not well-integrated (healthy) is dangerous because he or she occupies a position of authority towards other people. The effective manager has a high degree of self-knowledge, commitment to self care and managerial skills.

The effective manager has three general characteristics, as shown in Figure 2.2.

Management theory

This is a well thought-out rationale for why the manager behaves the way he or she does in order to accomplish tasks through the work of others.

Managing
self

General

Skills

Management
theory

Managerial
values

Self-management

Communication

Goal setting

Decision making

Problem solving

Conflict management

Figure 2.2

Managerial values

The effective manager knows what is worthwhile, what he or she should/ought to do. This is a type of personal philosophy that underlies personal goals.

Self management

The manager accepts responsibility and is resourceful in managing his or her time, stress, personal finances and career. The effective manager is actively involved in self care.

There are five vital skill areas that distinguish effective and ineffec-

tive managers. Each of these areas represents a set of skills. The
five are:

Communication

The effective manager is skilful in listening, self-expression, presenting information, and responding to the communications of
others. This skill set includes both oral and written communication.

Goal setting

The ability to establish clear objectives that are understood and
shared by others is a characteristic of effective managers. Working
well with both individuals and groups is required in this skill area.

Decision making

Effective managers are decisive, and they involve others whenever
appropriate. They have definite methods of making managerial
choices.

Problem solving

Effective managers are good at attacking problem situations creatively. They have the ability to sort through data, involve others
affected by the situation, and guide the solution-seeking process.

Conflict management

Effective management involves being able to intervene in difficult
situations between and among people. This requires courage,
sensitivity and skill in cutting through excess feeling to define issues
and push for negotiations. The effective manager does not aim for
conflict *resolution,* just a better contract.

This central area, managing self, is the most important set of
dimensions of effective managerial behaviour. If you want to be a
better manager, the place to start is with yourself.

Figure 2.3

MANAGING SUBORDINATES

The second ring of our model is managing subordinates. This involves one-to-one leadership, team development, evaluating employees' productivity, and developing and nurturing individuals. (See Figure 2.3.)

The manager has responsibilities not only to direct the work of others but also to develop them in the process. Effective managers know that it is good business to train his or her subordinates and to develop co-operation among them. The four following characteristics are important in determining effectiveness in this area.

Leadership style

The effective manager adapts his or her manner of influencing each individual according to that person's readiness to accomplish a given task. You might work with one person one way on one task and differently on another task. You might 'manage' two people differently doing the same task.

Team development

Effective managers acknowledge that people at work are inter-dependent and they look for ways to improve the ability of their subordinate group to work together better. Teamwork can result in higher commitment and better problem solving. This requires the manager to be able to influence group dynamics in a positive way.

Performance review

A good manager provides a clear, honest, growth-producing feed-back to his subordinates. People want to know, 'How am I doing?' An effective manager communicates with them straightforwardly not only on his evaluation of their productivity but also on expectations for specific improvements.

Coaching and counselling

The effective manager is skilful in developing individuals both in their ability to carry out job responsibilities and in their career and personal lives as well. Usually the manager is sensitive and helpful to the subordinate in finding ways of meeting his or her needs at work.

The crucial aspects of management effectiveness in the area of relating to subordinates are working well on a one-to-one basis and managing group dynamics.

MANAGING ORGANISATIONAL INTERFACES

The third ring of our model is managing organisational interfaces. This means working effectively on the interchanges between our unit and others whether they are above, at the same level or below.

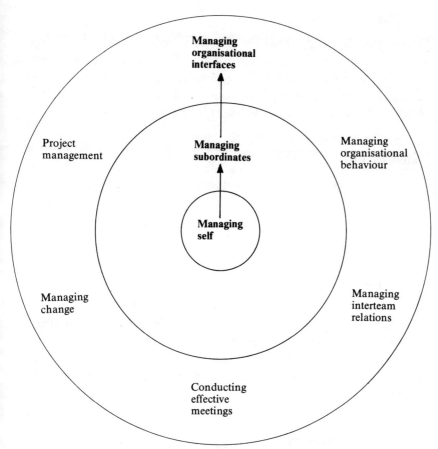

Figure 2.4

Many of these exchanges, of course, go on informally, but many are complicated by the bureaucratic structure and political networks of organisations. The five effectiveness areas which are important to consider are as follows. (See Figure 2.4.)

Managing organisational behaviour

Effective managers monitor and attempt to influence the organisation's values, goals, structure, climate and relationships. This means knowing how to work within the system both to improve it and use it non-manipulatively to attain the goals of their unit.

Managing interteam relations

Few organisational divisions can function completely independently. Managers have to interact with each other in order to maintain the integration of the system. Doing this effectively means taking the responsibility for and skilfully managing contacts between the managers' units and others.

Managing change

Good managers cope well with change rather than being managed by it. The most effective stance is proactive rather than reactive, making change happen in order to accomplish organisational objectives.

Project management

Many organisational activities involve cutting across unit boundaries. Skilful project managers are adept at generating inter-unit co-operation. (This area of responsibility is often critical in organisations that have a matrix structure in which there are functional departments that must co-ordinate their work on interdisciplinary projects.)

Conducting effective meetings

Most managers spend time leading or otherwise participating in meetings. Effective managers can contribute in a way which maximises the contribution of others. They can lead meetings which others find stimulating, enjoyable and useful. They know that poor meetings are not supported psychologically and that good meetings are an invaluable way of harnessing people's energy and support.

Since much of the interdepartmental co-ordination takes place in meetings, it is vitally important that the manager be skilful in conducting them. This means that to be effective the manager must be good at planning and conducting productive interchanges not only within his or her own staff area but also across organisational boundaries.

Effectiveness in managing the interfaces between one's unit and other organisational parts is necessary for ensuring that the system remains integrated and that individual managers do not insulate themselves unduly.

MANAGING EXTERNAL RELATIONS

The final effectiveness level is managing external relations. This refers to the areas of responsibility that the manager has *vis-à-vis* people outside the organisation, such as customers, clients, suppliers, potential employees and the general public. On the graphic model we show this outside the circles in order to symbolise external relations.

There are three important skill areas to take into account when considering how effectively the manager conducts external relations. (See Figure 2.5.)

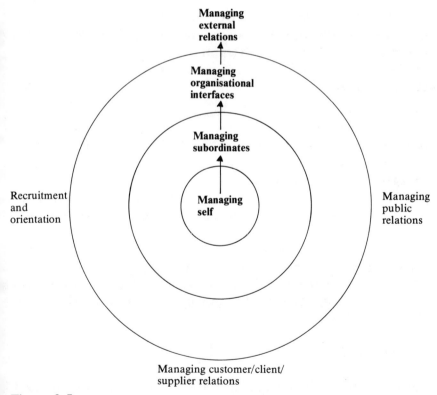

Figure 2.5

Managing public relations

Good managers are public relations-oriented. They make certain that all contacts with the world outside the organisation are handled in ways that are beneficial to the organisation. This means that the effective manager is skilful in public speaking, relating to the press, representing the organisation at public functions and greeting visitors.

Managing customer/client/supplier relations

This area of responsibility is not equally important to all managers, but for some it is a large part of their everyday relationships. The effective manager works at meeting outside needs while maintaining the integration of his or her own system.

Recruitment and orientation

Even though these functions are often carried out by people in the personnel department, almost all the managers have responsibilities in interviewing and on-the-job training. Effective managers understand that the computer saying, 'Garbage in, garbage out', can also refer to human resources.

Effectiveness in management, then, extends beyond the boundary of the organisation. Human systems have always been flexible. People spend more time outside the workplace than within it, and they are constantly interacting with various individuals and groups. Good managers are sensitive to the need to monitor and influence the quality of these interactions in order to meet the needs of the organisation. Most organisations have become 'glasshouses' in the sense that there is often outside intrusion, i.e. from customers and clients, governmental regulatory agencies, suppliers, public pressure groups, labour organisations, professional associations, etc.

In order to be effective the manager must take all of this into account in making decisions and solving problems within his or her administrative unit.

THE FULL MODEL

The twenty dimensions of managerial effectiveness are summarised in the full model. (See Figure 2.6.) Of course, managers are not

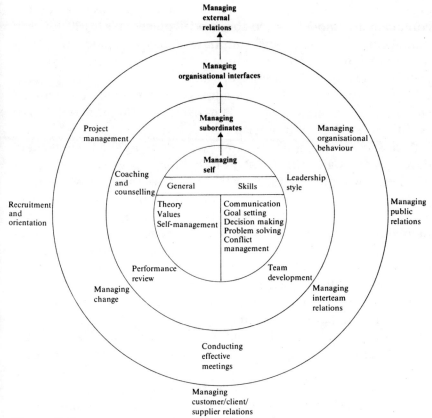

Figure 2.6

equally effective or ineffective in all of these areas. Some are more important than others, however. We believe that the closer to the centre the more important the skill. That is, if you want to be a better manager, work on yourself first, improve relationships with your subordinates, improve how your department works with others, and then concentrate on the quality of your contacts with outsiders. Growth and development begins at home, so to speak.

USE OF THE COMPETENCY MODEL

One immediate use of this model is to evaluate the content of management development programmes. In other words, specialists in management development can analyse the topics included in all of their courses, seminars and workshops in order to determine the degree to which their aggregate coverage matches that of the competencies model. Since the model places a priority on self management, a programme's emphases can be compared also. How much of what is touched on in the programme's offerings concentrates on developing the manager's ability to be an effective person? Of course, the model does not address itself to technical content, such as finance, marketing, etc. The coverage of these areas has to be evaluated according to other models.

A closely related analysis can also be done by the management development staff. This involves individuals assessing themselves on their own preparedness with regard to the twenty areas of competence. The staff may discover some blind spots, or areas in which they either need to develop expertise themselves or to add to their staff persons who have these competencies. Such an analysis could have a highly beneficial teambuilding effect among the staff of management development specialists. To facilitate such a study, a simple checklist is provided at the end of this chapter.

A third use of the managerial competencies model is to use it as a guide for developing such a model within the organisation.

Several processes can be used for these purposes. The management development staff can study our model and develop their own according to their own experience, in a manner similar to our own method. Interviews can be held with managers to determine what they believe to be critical competencies, and these opinions can be integrated into a model that is unique to the organisation. A survey questionnaire can be constructed from our list in order to determine what managers believe to be important competencies needed to fulfil their responsibilities. Training sessions can be conducted in which managers construct their own competency models. A simplified discussion of developing theoretical models is provided by Pfeiffer and Jones (1980). Our experience with the latter method has been that managers become intensively involved in the process and almost inevitably assess themselves during the activity.

Model-based training needs assessment is obviously preferable to unsystematic study of management development priorities. Our competency model lends itself easily to such a use, as we discuss in detail in the next chapter.

Finally, this model can become part of the content of the management development programme. The model can be introduced through lecture-discussion or self-assessment by instrumentation.

REFERENCES

Mintzberg, H. *The Nature of Managerial Work.* New York: Harper & Row, 1973.

Pfeiffer, J. W., and Jones, J. E. (Eds) *The 1980 Annual Handbook for Group Facilitators.* San Diego, California: University Associates, 1980, pp. 171–4.

MANAGER SELF-ASSESSMENT CHECKLIST

Effectiveness area	I'm OK on this	I need to learn more about this	This does not apply to me
Managing self			
Theory of management ...			
Values			
Self-management			
Communication			
Goal setting			
Decision making			
Problem solving			
Conflict management ...			
Managing subordinates			
Leadership style			
Team development			
Performance review			
Coaching and counselling			
Managing organisational interfaces			
Managing organisational behaviour			
Managing interteam relations			
Conducting effective meetings			
Managing change			
Project management			
Managing external relations			
Managing public relations			
Managing customers/ client/supplier relations			
Recruitment and orientation			

3 Assessing developmental needs

In order to plan for and design management development programmes that can have a beneficial impact both on individuals and
on the organisation, it is necessary for some form of research to
be carried out on the recipients of such activities. Somehow managers
have to be studied with regard to what they need to learn in order
to perform their task functions competently. This chapter is concerned with the why and how of training needs assessment. We will
also look at some principles that pertain to the process of determining
the needs of managers for development. Two instruments based on
our managerial competencies model will be included. These instruments – one a survey, the other a structured interview – effectively
put this assessment process into action.

It is important at this stage to define what we understand by 'a
training need'. Morrison (1976) says:

> A *training need* may be described as existing any time an actual
> condition differs from a desired condition in the human, or
> 'people', aspect of organization performance or, more specifi-
> cally, when a change in present human knowledges, skills, or
> attitudes can bring about the desired performance (p. 9–1).

So a developmental need is a gap between what exists now and what
is desired in managerial behaviour. Ways of uncovering the gaps
that may be keeping management from performing optimally are
called assessment strategies. It is important that management
development personnel approach the assessment of learning needs
carefully and systematically, for two main reasons. Firstly, studying

managers in an action-research mode can control the biases of trainers. When we assume that we know what others need to learn, our programmes are often based on projections. Secondly, involving managers in determining priorities for management development increases the likelihood that they will support activities that flow out of the assessment. In other words, they are more prone to develop a sense of 'ownership' over the programme if they feel influential in shaping its emphases. Since management development programmes require committed participants for their success, it is important to reflect that this requires active participation. Jones (1981) states,

> ... members of the organization need to be a part of the process if the are expected to be committed to its outcomes ... Meaningful participation leads to a sense of involvement; this evokes a feeling of influence that generates psychological ownership, which leads to *commitment*. There is no shortcut to commitment; it evolves within individuals as a result of their perception of themselves as influential (p. 157).

In order for managers to take full advantage of the opportunities offered them in a management development programme, they need to feel committed. Having them participate in studies that provide guidance to the trainer(s) is an essential strategy in ensuring their support and hopefully their attendance.

At different stages of their careers managers have different development needs. Early in their careers they are more engrossed in technical activities, and they take on more supervisory and leadership responsibilities as they progress. Margerison (1978, 1979) found that the two broad types of activities – technical and managerial – had an almost straight-line relationship to each other in the course of a manager's career. Figure 3.1 shows that as one develops more experience, managerial activities take on more and more importance and that technical activities lessen in the amount of time they require.

Our managerial competencies model does not include technical activities, since it is our firm belief that almost all persons who are promoted to supervisory responsibilities are capable technically. That is, they more or less know the jobs of the people whose behaviour they will manage. Unfortunately, it seems equally true that few managers are well prepared for the non-technical, human relations aspects of the supervisory position. Accordingly, we have placed our emphasis on conceptualising and operationalising a model of

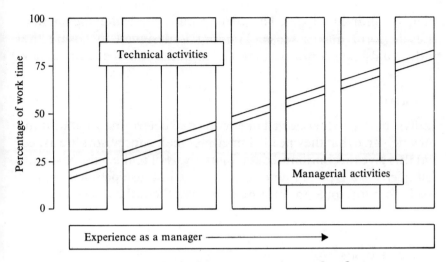

Figure 3.1   Margerison's findings on career trends of managers

what managers are likely to need to learn in order to excel as managers, not as technicians.

MODES OF NEEDS ASSESSMENT

Four major approaches to determining what managers need to learn have evolved in management development. These are organisational analysis, job analysis, 'felt' needs, and mixed methods. The first three are 'pure' types, and the fourth is eclectic. Jones (1979) described these approaches in a conference on human resource development.

Organisational analysis

A study of the needs of the total system can be the basis for designing training. 'What skills and knowledge do we need to manufacture widgets (teach young people to read, help people become less dependent on drugs, etc.)?' This type of analysis begins with a priority being placed on organisational output, working backwards to an assessment of present human resources, and designing training to fill the gaps.

Job analysis

Here the emphasis is on studying the knowledge and skill requirements of individual jobs. The assumption is made that the job in its present form makes sense. Training is designed to ensure that individuals can perform at least at minimal levels of proficiency.

Felt needs

Individuals are interviewed or surveyed to determine what training they perceive that they need. Sometimes their supervisors are asked, but this gives secondhand data for analysis of real needs. Assessing felt needs is a type of marketing strategy, because people are more likely to participate in training that gives them the assistance they want.

Mixed methods

Designing training based on multiple assessments from different vantage points capitalises on the assets of each method while avoiding its potential disadvantages. For example, the organisation may require negotiation skills, the job may require third-party intervention skills, and the individual may want help on coping with change. Training in this situation could be fashioned to address all three needs. Both organisational analysis and job analysis typically focus on performance and neglect affective needs. An assessment of felt needs can be overly personalised, losing the job and system focus, so too much attention can be placed on systems. Mixed methods attempt to keep these priorities in balance.

MD and OD

We make a sharp distinction between *management* development (MD) and *organisation* development (OD), and we believe that it is important to do so. In needs assessment it is critical to stay away from the assessment of organisational problems and to focus on managerial behaviour. In conducting an organisational analysis, then, the focus must be on determining what managers need to learn in order for the system to behave effectively. Training and organisation development have many similarities, among which are the following:

1   The two activities have the same meta-goal – improved organisational functioning.

2   Both activities focus on balancing concerns between individual needs and organisational demands.
3   They are both subsumed under the umbrella of human resource development.
4   Both training and OD feature applications of behavioural science to human and system problems.
5   The two types of effort have a common value base.
6   They are very often carried out by the same people.

On the other hand, it is important to recognise that management development and OD differ in significant ways. These differences have clear implications for guiding the assessment of management learning needs. The chief differences between these two programmes are as follows:

1   The 'target' for management development is the individual manager; in OD it is groups of people and systems.
2   Management development requires that its practitioners have skills in presentation and facilitation of learning; OD calls for skills in system assessment, problem identification, problem solving, and intervention.
3   The role of the professional in management development is that of a 'shaper' of learning, but the primary role of the OD practitioner is process consultation.
4   Management development specialists engage in training needs assessment, designing, and conducting courses; OD people involve themselves in action research and consulting with groups and individuals about problems.
5   The content of management development courses centres around simulated problems, but OD focuses exclusively on real ones.

In carrying out an organisational analysis, then, one should pay attention to what the system needs from the individual manager and avoid using training as a substitute for OD.

Job analysis focuses on task functions rather than on the person. Five methods of studying management jobs were outlined by the Food, Drink and Tobacco Industry Training Board (undated, pp. 14–15): job description, key job features, main problems, critical incidents, and time allocation. Job descriptions contain valuable information for needs assessment, such as job definition, major areas of responsibility, objectives of the job, and measurement criteria for job performance. Studying job descriptions, however, tends to place inordinate emphasis on the technical requirements of the job, so management requirements are necessary also. Analysing key job features involves asking managers to report on their own chief responsibilities. Studying main problems requires managers to assess their own chronic concerns in task functions. Time allocation requires managers to report, usually through diaries, on how they utilise this resource.

Felt needs analysis is more highly subjective than are organisational and job analyses. Here, in effect, we ask managers what help they would like in order to gain more job satisfaction. Obviously, in the light of the earlier discussion it is important not to permit the analysis of self perceived needs to change into data-gathering on what may be wrong with the organisation. In the next section of this chapter we will present two reproducible instruments that are designed to control and focus the amount of subjectivity that trainers receive in the assessment of felt needs. It is our view that model-based assessment gives the management development specialist clarity in interpreting the data and translating it into programme planning.

PRINCIPAL ASSESSMENT METHODS

In conducting a training needs assessment management development personnel typically use four methods: study of documents, observation, interviews, and surveys. Organisational and job analyses involve the study of documents primarily, but they may also entail interviews. Study of felt needs relies heavily on interview and survey methods.

The training needs interview worksheet

This is a guide to be used by the management development specialist in conversations with individual managers. The theory for the interview is our managerial competencies model. The trainer takes notes on the form itself, so copies need to be duplicated for this purpose. After the set of interviews is completed, the data are collated, item by item, for trend or theme analysis.

Setting up an interview schedule involves selecting interviewees, orienting them, conducting the interviews and analysing the results. Selection is best done, in our judgement, either randomly or randomly within management levels. This makes it possible to get a representative 'feel' for what managers need without having to bear the expense of interviewing everyone. Of course, it also obviates getting the biased view that other selection methods (such as friends, or people who are conveniently accessible) might develop.

Conducting 'felt need' interviews needs to be done in a way that increases the rapport between management and management development. The training needs interview worksheet contains several tips on opening and closing the conversation. It also has reminders for the interviewer to check understanding of what is being said. For further discussion of how to carry out these interviews, see Jones (1973).

The management development priorities form

This survey form is also built on our managerial competencies model. It is a questionnaire that involves a linear, 5-point scale of self-assessment in thirty-two needs areas as defined by the model. There is space for managers to specify additional areas of training needs. This form is intended to be used with all managers, more or less simultaneously. The management development staff provide an individual copy for each manager, complete with a covering letter. They also provide a means of returning their responses and eventually collate and analyse the ratings. The management development priorities summary form gives a useful means of recording the results of the tally. On this summary form the management development specialist records the average rating for each of the thirty-two items. Then the averages are rank ordered from 1, the area of greatest need, to 32, the area of least self-perceived need.

NEEDS ASSESSMENT CONSIDERATIONS

In conducting studies of the developmental needs of managers it is important to proceed methodically and carefully. In this section we discuss what we believe to be critical considerations in planning and carrying out such research.

Do not assess needs you cannot meet. It is tempting to ask managers about many 'what if' options. If the programme cannot accommodate a wide range of learning priorities, then the assessment has to be narrowed to those areas on which the staff is competently prepared and for which time and other resources can be made available.

Do not assess to many needs at once. Unless the programme is being initiated or extensively modified, it is best to limit the needs assessment to those options that are viable in the short term. It is permissible to conduct comprehensive assessment when it is made plain to managers that the data will be used in long-range programme planning.

Be aware that the needs assessment process raises expectations. The act of interviewing and surveying managers on their needs implies that the needs that they identify will somehow be met. Unless the programme is flexible enough to address the entire range of felt needs of potential participants, it is wise to ask about a limited array of possibilities and respond to the trends in the data – visibly and promptly.

Awareness of need can be a learning. Helping managers to determine what they need to learn can give them a new perspective on their preparedness for implementing their job responsibilities. Training needs assessment interviews can be encounters within which managers engage in self-exploration that can lead to their clarifying for themselves what they need to learn in order to direct their careers more effectively.

Be aware of those who are not a part of the action. People whose needs are not assessed can be expected to be less supportive of management development programming than those who supply the priorities. This means both personnel below and above those being assessed. It may be necessary to keep these groups who are outside the scope of the assessment informed of the aims, scope, and emphases of the research in order to prevent their undermining the management development effort.

'Big oaks from little acorns grow'. In planning management development programmes or programme improvements it is important to begin small and work slowly. Wholesale changes can be disruptive to the system and hard to 'sell'. A good strategy is to begin with the most critical needs or gaps and proceed step-by-step to the less pressing ones. Managers are more likely to respond favourably to 'symptom relief', for help with chronic headaches they face every day.

Do not ask one what another needs. One basic mistake that management development professionals make sometimes is to ask supervisors what their supervisees need to learn. This practice can not only generate misleading and inaccurate data, it can also fail to capitalise on the principle discussed earlier – commitment through meaningful participation. In our judgement the best source of information on training needs is the group of potential training participants themselves.

A need does not constitute a market; it is a potential one. Unless managers ask for help in a particular area, they are possibly unlikely to be receptive to offered developmental opportunities. It is of little or no interest that someone else views them as needing help in the area. Creating a market for a need is expensive. Management development specialists should be cautious, in our view, of introducing training that managers do not themselves see a need for.

Managers often do not know what they need; many deny their developmental deficiencies. It is unsafe to assume that managers are completely valid reporters of their learning needs. That is why it is critical to balance felt needs with organisational and job analysis in the needs assessment. Also, it is critical to assess the needs of a significant number of managers to make sure that their self reports are representative of the cadre of leaders.

Training is not always the answer. Sometimes training needs assessment uncovers organisational 'hot spots' that need attention, and often conducting training sessions is not a relevant, straightforward response to the situation. It behoves management development personnel to respond to these disclosures in resourceful ways – sometimes with interventions that are more directly confrontive than training.

Make a sharp distinction between training and OD. Pfeiffer and Jones (1976) indicate that training, education and OD are different activities. Reilly (1973) spells out clear differences between the two activities. We have discussed these distinctions earlier in this chapter, but the point begs for emphasis: training needs assessment focuses exclusively on management development and not organisational behaviour.

TRAINING NEEDS INTERVIEW WORKSHEET

Interviewer .... Interviewee Code Number..........
Date .... Time .... Location ....

Instructions

Use this worksheet to record, *in the interviewee's own words,* responses
to the following general questions. Keep control of the interview,
since you have the task of gathering information. Paraphrase from
time to time to demonstrate that you are understanding what is said.
Ask for clarification when you do not understand. Keep the focus on
training needs, not system problems.

Opening the interview

Make the following points, in your own words: (a) that you are
interviewing a representative cross-section of managers; (b) for the
purpose of assessing their needs for management development; (c)
that the data will be pooled for establishing priorities, anonymously;
and then ask them to answer the following questions, candidly.

1   There have been many theories of management proposed. In
     recent years, there has been a lot of interest in Japanese
     theories. How interested are you in learning further about these
     models?

2   Many observers of organisational behaviour have pointed out
     that often managers and their subordinates have different
     personal values. What is your view, and would you want to
     explore this situation in a training setting?

3   Self-management involves the management of your time, the
     stresses you experience, your personal finances and your career.
     What interest do you have in getting some help on each of
     these?

Time management

Stress management

Personal financial management

Managing your career

4   Communication skills are important to us all. They involve listening, self-expression, presenting information and written communication. What training would you like to have to keep up your communication skills?

5   Individual and group goal-setting is an area common to all managers. What do you see as a need for you in this activity?

6   When and how to involve others in decision making is a critical managerial consideration. How interested are you in attending training in this area?

7   If there were no problems, we probably wouldn't need managers. We have some problem-solving models we could incorporate into a training course. How helpful would that be for you?

8   Managing situations in which people are in conflict with each other involves a set of trainable skills and strategies. What is your level of interest in learning how to manage such situations more effectively?

9   How you manage your subordinates is often referred to as your leadership style. We have some training activities that can help you to learn how to maximise the impact of your style. To what degree would that be helpful to you?

10   Many managers want their subordinates to work together as a team. How much interest do you have in learning methods of generating higher co-operation within your work unit?

11   Reviewing subordinates' performance is a necessary part of any manager's job. We have training that can help you to turn this activity into a way of making your employees more responsible. How much would this be helpful to you?

12 You have to help to develop each of your subordinates and two aspects of that effort are coaching them on job skills and counselling with them on their careers and personal development. How interested are you in attending training on these activities?

Coaching

Counselling

13 We all do our work in the context of the larger organisation. How interested are you in studying the dynamics of organisational behaviour, from a managerial perspective?

14 Your workgroup (department, division, etc.) has relationships with other units in the organisation. Often there is friction between groups. How helpful would training in managing inter-team relations be to you?

15 About the only thing that we can definitely count on around here is that things will change. What is your interest in attending training that focuses on managing change effectively?

16   Sometimes the projects that people like you manage cut across organisational boundaries. How helpful would training be to you in project management?

17   You spend a lot of your time planning, conducting and participating in meetings. We have some training that could be helpful to you on this topic. Do you feel you could use some help in managing meetings effectively?

18   All of us have public relations responsibilities, whether we recognise them or not. How interested are you in participating in training in these areas?

Public speaking

Relating to the press

Representing the organisation at public functions

Greeting visitors

19 Many managers spend a lot of time taking care of relationships with clients, customers and suppliers. How helpful would training in this area be to you?

20 Almost all managers here have at least some responsibility in recruitment, interviewing job applicants and job orientation. What is your training need in each of these activities?

Recruitment

Interviewing job applicants

Job orientation

21 In what other areas that I haven't asked about do you feel the need for training?

Closing the interview

Make the following points in your own words: (a) thank them for their openness; (b) tell them that you will pool the information you have received to set training priorities; (c) assure them that they will not be quoted by name; and (d) that they will hear the results of this needs assessment from the training department in the near future.

MANAGEMENT DEVELOPMENT PRIORITIES

John E. Jones and Mike Woodcock

Code:

Instructions

This brief questionnaire will greatly help in planning training for persons like you in our organisation. Respond to each item below as it relates to you as a manager. Do not indicate what training others need, only yourself. Think of what knowledge and skills you need to perform your job competently and what training you would like to receive in preparing yourself for promotion or a new managerial assignment. Your answers will be pooled with others' to develop priorities in our management development programme. You will not be identified individually in the results. You will receive a report of the outcomes of this survey as soon as we can compile them.

Use the following scale to indicate your training needs:

I have a definite need for training in this area;	5
This kind of training would probably be helpful to me;	4
I am undecided or uncertain about this for me;	3
This training would probably not be useful for me;	2
I definitely do not need training in this management area;	1

Write the appropriate rating-scale number in the box at the end of each item.

1   How to adapt modern theories of management to the situations I face on my job.   ☐
2   How to take personal values – my own and others – into account as I manage the work of my subordinates and make my own personal choices.   ☐
3   How to manage my time effectively.   ☐
4   How to cope effectively with the stress I experience on the job.   ☐
5   How to manage my personal finances effectively.   ☐
6   How to manage the development of my own career.   ☐
7   How to listen to people better.   ☐
8   How to express myself better orally.   ☐
9   How to improve my written communications.   ☐

10 How t⸱   ⁱ presentations of information, both
    forma.   .al, more effectively.   ☐
11 How to se⸱ ⸱ s effectively, both individually and in
    groups.   ☐
12 How to manage the participation of subordinates in
    decision making.   ☐
13 How to solve problems, with creativity and commitment. ☐
14 How to manage situations in which people are in conflict
    with each other   ☐
15 How to adapt my leadership style to the demands of the
    task and the needs of my subordinates.   ☐
16 How to develop more teamwork within my work group.   ☐
17 How to make performance reviews work for me in making
    my subordinates more responsible.   ☐
18 How to coach my employees effectively on their job
    performance.   ☐
19 How to counsel with my people on their personal problems. ☐
20 How to understand how organisational behaviour affects
    my job.   ☐
21 How to manage the interfaces between my group and
    others in the organisation.   ☐
22 How to manage change effectively, rather than be managed
    by it.   ☐
23 How to manage interdepartmental projects effectively.   ☐
24 How to conduct effective meetings.   ☐
25 How to speak in public effectively.   ☐
26 How to manage my relations with members of the press.   ☐
27 How to represent the organisation effectively at public
    functions.   ☐
28 How to greet visitors.   ☐
29 How to improve my relationships with clients, customers,
    and suppliers.   ☐
30 How to recruit employees effectively.   ☐
31 How to conduct effective interviews with job applicants.   ☐
32 How to orientate new employees and their transfer to their
    jobs.   ☐
33 (Other training needs) _____
34 _____
35 _____

Thank you for your co-operation. You will receive a survey report
soon.

MANAGEMENT DEVELOPMENT PRIORITIES
SUMMARY FORM

Rating scale
5 Definitely need   4 Probably need
3 Uncertain   2 Probably not need
1 Definitely not need

Group: No:

	Effectiveness category	Item number	Average rating	Rank order
Level 1 Managing Self — Personal Management	Management theory	1		
	Managerial values	2		
	Time	3		
	Stress	4		
	Personal finances	5		
	Career	6		
Communication	Listening	7		
	Self expression	8		
	Written	9		
	Oral presentation	10		
	Goal setting	11		
	Decision making	12		
	Problem solving	13		
	Managing conflict	14		
Level 2 Managing Subordinates	Leadership style	15		
	Team leadership	16		
	Performance review	17		
	Coaching	18		
	Counselling	19		
Level 3 Managing Organisational Interfaces	Managing organisational behaviour	20		
	Managing interteam relations	21		
	Managing change	22		
	Project management	23		
	Conducting effective meetings	24		

MANAGEMENT DEVELOPMENT PRIORITIES
SUMMARY FORM (continued)

	Effectiveness category	Item number	Average rating	Rank order
Level 4 Managing External Relations — Public Relations	Public speaking	25		
	Press relations	26		
	Representing organisation	27		
	Greeting visitors	28		
	Customer/client/supplier relationships	29		
Recruitment/Orientation	Recruitment	30		
	Interviewing applicants	31		
	Orientation	32		
(Other)				

REFERENCES

Atwood, L. T., 'Management Development in British Companies', *JEIT,* vol. 3 no. 8, 1979, pp. 1–32.

Jones, J. E., 'The Sensing Interview', pp. 213–24 in J. E. Jones and J. W. Pfeiffer (eds) *The 1973 Annual Handbook for Group Facilitators,* San Diego, CA: University Associates, 1973.

Jones, J. E., 'Experiential Training: Status and Promise', *Group and Organization Studies,* September, 1979, vol. 4, no. 3, pp. 294–300.

Jones, J. E., 'The Organizational Universe', pp. 155–64 in J. E. Jones and J. W. Pfeiffer (eds) *The 1981 Annual Handbook for Group Facilitators,* San Diego, CA: University Associates, 1981.

Management Training and Development, London: Food Drink and Tobacco Industry Training Board (undated).

Margerison, C. J., 'Making Tomorrow's Managers', *Management Today,* May, 1978.

Margerison, C. J., 'Highway to Managerial Success', *Personnel Management,* IPM, August, 1979.

Morrison, J. H., 'Determining Training Needs', in R. L. Craig (ed.) *Training and Development Handbook,* 2nd ed, New York: McGraw Hill, 1976, pp. 9–1 through 9–17.

Mumford, Alan, 'The Role of the External Consultant', in E. B. Taylor and G. L. Lippitt (eds) *Management Development and Training Handbook,* London: McGraw-Hill, 1975.

Pfeiffer, J. W., and Jones, J. E., 'A current assessment of OD: What it is and why it often fails', pp. 225–32, in J. W. Pfeiffer and J. E. Jones (eds) *The 1976 Annual Handbook for Group Facilitators,* San Diego, CA: University Associates, 1976.

Reilly, A. J., 'Three approaches to organizational learning', pp. 130–31 in J. E. Jones and J. W. Pfeiffer (eds) *The 1973 Annual Handbook for Group Facilitators,* San Diego, CA: University Associates, 1973.

4 Designing management development courses

The effectiveness of management development is most dependent on the quality of the courses offered to managers. Three aspects of these courses are important to consider – content, design and instructor style. The content must be relevant to the work that participants do in their jobs, the design of the course should involve participants actively in managing their own learning, and the training style of the facilitator needs to be compatible with the preferred learning styles of participants. These three quality dimensions are interdependent; that is, the total impact of the course is affected by all three. The importance of each determinant and their interrelatedness can be illustrated by a three-legged stool. (See Figure 4.1.) If any of the three 'legs' of the stool is deficient, the entire structure is unstable.

Needs assessment, done properly, leads to making sure that the courses are consistent with the general principles of adult learning,

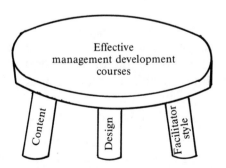

Figure 4.1

which ensures that the method will 'deliver the goods'. A good course needs good staffing, however, and the effectiveness of instruction is largely due to the appropriateness of the instructors' styles. We discussed how to conduct training needs assessments in Chapter 3.

In this chapter we will explore how to design courses consistent with learning objectives, principles of andragogy (adult learning), and appropriateness of method. Chapter 5 will focus on the 'third leg of the stool' – facilitator style.

It is our firm belief that courses need detailed advanced planning. We are equally convinced that facilitators need to expect to change the design during the course itself. In this chapter we will outline a step-by-step procedure for designing management development courses. We will include an instrument for making an inventory of the resources available for a given course. Then we will introduce the notion of assessing the preferred learning styles of participants and present an instrument for that purpose. Since managers are adults, we will review adult learning principles and their implications for course design. We will discuss the appropriateness of various training technologies and will include a worksheet that facilitates selecting appropriate means to realise course objectives. The chapter will conclude with a consideration of how to plan the opening and closing of course sessions.

A COURSE DESIGN PROCEDURE

In order to ensure that a given management development course is of the highest standard possible, we propose to design a procedure that has seventeen stages. We will discuss the rationale for each step separately. Then we will point out the advantages of the overall approach.

1 *Assess the learning needs of managers who are expected to attend.* This topic was explored in depth in the previous chapter. The primary concern here is to diagnose needs in ways that make prospective participants feel influential with regard to the priorities for their learning. Also, the content emphases of the course must be seen as relevant by the participants.

2 *Inventory the resources available for planning and conducting the course.* To combat the tendency to have a 'solution in search of a problem' and to make sure that the planning is thorough, it is

important to take stock of what you have to work with in design. In the next section of this chapter we will include a worksheet for this purpose.

3 *Assess the learning styles of participants and instructors.* Managers differ in how they interact with each other in training settings and how they prefer to acquire information. The learning style assessment inventory, included later in this chapter, is designed to facilitate surveying the cognitive and interactive styles of the persons who will be present in the course.

4 *Establish course objectives.* Our bias is to state these in a general way, to allow for learning through discovery. Specifying goals in micro is a useful discipline for skills, but the activity is far less useful in the areas of attitude development and understanding of concepts.

5 *Reflect on principles of adult learning and their implications for course design.* Later in this chapter we will outline sixteen characteristics of adults as learners and what to do to make course design take the principles into account. What is clear is that strategies, tactics, and techniques that are effective for teaching children cannot be simply extrapolated to training/educating adult managers.

6 *Select appropriate training technologies for each objective.* Later in this chapter we will include a discussion of common technologies and a worksheet for matching them to course goals. Since management development personnel tend to 'talk at' participants too much in our experience, this planning approach should lead to a thoughtful consideration of how to treat each objective.

7 *Prepare a time chart for the course.* We have found it helpful to create a chart on which we will lay out the entire course design on one page. This facilitates allocating time for various content areas and planning for such things as recreation, time alone for participants etc. Time charts also remind us to consider the probable cumulative effects of training activities on the energy/attention level of participants.

8 *Decide how much time will be given to each primary objective.* Not all course objectives can be segmented into time frames since they cut across all of the activities of the course, but it is important to determine how much coverage primary content areas will receive. This practice will make it easier to consider the feasibility of achieving course goals.

9 *Arrange the content into useful topical blocks.* There should be some logic (or 'psychologic') for the sequence of course themes. It is almost always useful to present the rationale for the topic sequence and the interrelatedness of the content areas in the opening session of the course. This gives participants a kind of cognitive roadmap that can be useful in guiding the integration of their learning.

10 *Assess group development activities.* It is important to plan for diagnosing the adequacy of the learning experience from time to time during the course. This helps to ensure that the course meets the expectations of participants and to facilitate managers' sharing responsibility for the maintenance of the learning community. At the very least, some 'mid-course correction' diagnosis and negotiation needs to be included.

11 *Emphasise the opening and closing sessions.* We firmly believe that these two sessions are the most important strategically for the facilitator. The first clears expectations, sets standards for behaviour in the course, enlists participants in managing their learning and begins to create a feeling of community within the group. The last 'finishes unfinished business', commits learners to applying their new knowledge and skills and inspires managers to follow through. We will discuss how to design these two sessions in the last section of this chapter.

12 *Arrange 'energisers' in spots in which participants are likely to be experiencing drag.* These are change-of-pace activities that usually involve physical movement. They are often content-free, fun, and competitive. Consider including them just after lunch, during long sessions, and just before important changes in topic.

13 *Arrange applications-planning activities.* We favour the 'buddy system', establishing helping pairs within the participant group during the goal-setting phase of the opening session. Partners then meet after all the main learning events to plan applications to their 'back home' work situations. We believe that it is highly desirable for applications planning to be organised as a continuous activity throughout the course, not just at the end.

14 *Fill-in activities to cover all objectives.* It is useful to plan variety into the sequence of events that are intended to achieve each objective. This is the step that incorporates the results of the analysis that was carried out in step 6 of this procedure. We began at the two ends of the course. Now we fill in the middle.

15 *Schedule staff sessions for during-course design modifications.* A basic principle of designing courses is to plan to change the design during the delivery of the experience. A related principle is to over-design, that is to develop back-up designs that are based on contingency planning. During the course itself the staff needs to assess how well the design is working and effect modifications. In our experience it is best to schedule most of these meetings beforehand. We also hold the belief that these meetings should be open to course participants.

16 *Solicit critiques of the design before conducting the course.* Sometimes the course designer has a blindspot that others can see but that he or she cannot. Colleagues may also be useful in checking the tendency to use 'favourite' techniques or models in several courses. When we ask another person to criticise our course design, we should be able to be articulate about its rationale, since we shall have to explain it to the participants.

17 *Prepare/assemble materials and equipment.* This involves developing handouts, audiovisuals, worksheets, etc. They should be adapted to the realities being faced by managers in the organisation, and they should be duplicated to appear professional. In Chapter 6 we shall discuss logistical planning, but it is important to begin assembling equipment as soon as the course design has been prepared.

   This course design procedure seems at first glance to be cumbersome and detailed. We maintain, however, that something like it is necessary for effective management development to take place in the training room. The sequence can be modified to fit various organisational situations, but some approximation of each of the steps should be considered. It is useful to remember the principle of five p's: 'poor planning precedes poor performance'.

INVENTORY DESIGN RESOURCES

Before designing a management development course it is desirable to conduct a systematic assessment of what there is to work with. This effort helps us to be comprehensive in planning and to test the feasibility of achieving the objectives we have set for the course. If we do not find sufficient resources we either have to scale down our expectations for course outcomes or work towards the creation of adequate resources.

Four initial considerations are necessary in determining course resources: participants, time, staff and support. Who shows up to take the course has a profound influence on the quality of the learning experience. The time blocks available to conduct the course constitute critical parameters. The availability of qualified instructional staff determines what can be expected to be achieved during the course. Some designs require a lot of audiovisual equipment and materials, budget, clerical back-up, etc.

The course design resource worksheet is intended to be used during step 2 of the course design procedure. It can be utilised individually or by staff teams to discuss not only what the course parameters are but also what concerns the staff has about each. This analysis should lead to action planning on increasing resources, setting realistic course objectives, and designing appropriate course activities.

COURSE DESIGN RESOURCES WORKSHEET

Instructions

The purpose of this form is to assist in preparing a course design by taking an inventory of those resources that can be used in delivering a worthwhile learning experience. Use the worksheet creatively, i.e. adapt it to fit your management development situation. Not all courses require all of the resources listed.

Participants

Answer – My concerns

1 How many will participate in the course? _____ _____

2 How many organisational levels will be represented? _____ _____

3 How well are they acquainted with each other? _____ _____

4 How much previous training in this general topical training area have they previously received? _____ _____

5 What percentage am I personally acquainted with? _____ _____

6 To what degree will they bring valuable, relevant work experience in the topic area? _____ _____

7 To what degree will there be opportunities for them actually to use what they learn when they return to the job? _____ _____

8 How much support and reinforcement will the organisation give them to improve their work effectiveness? _____ _____

9 How will participants be selected? _____ _____

10 How will participants be oriented to the course? _____ _____

Staff

11 Are there qualified co-trainers avail-
    able for the course?   _____   _____

12 To what extent can line managers be
    used as instructors during the course?   _____   _____

13 To what degree are adjunct staff
    effective in using interactive instruc-
    tional methods?   _____   _____

14 Is there a 'continuity person' available
    to ensure that the work of instructors
    is co-ordinated?   _____   _____

15 Are course instructors held account-
    able for the quality of the learning
    experience?   _____   _____

16 To what extent do staff members have
    credibility in the subject area?   _____   _____

17 How interpersonally compatible are
    the staff?   _____   _____

18 Can we afford to use 'outside' people
    on the staff?   _____   _____

Time

19 How much time can be allotted to the
    course itself?   _____   _____

20 Can the time be taken as an entity or
    must it be spread out over several
    sessions?   _____   _____

21 How much participant pre-work is
    feasible?   _____   _____

22 What will be the length of daily
    sessions?   _____   _____

23 Will there be a 'jet-lag factor' to
    consider in the opening session?   _____   _____

24 Will the course session need to be completed in time for participant travel? _____ _____

25 Is there enough time to have a reasonable expectation of achieving course objectives? _____ _____

Supports

26 To what degree are materials and handouts readily available for the course? _____ _____

27 To what degree must materials be adapted/written/prepared for the course? _____ _____

28 To what degree must permissions be sought to duplicate copyrighted material? _____ _____

29 Will there be stenographic and reproduction facilities available during the course? _____ _____

30 To what degree must the training site be adapted? _____ _____

31 How adequate are the audiovisual supports (projects, flipcharts, videotape equipment, recorders, etc)? _____ _____

32 How much money is budgeted to support this course? _____ _____

33 Are there organisational and/or community sites available to be visited and studied during the course? _____ _____

34 How can computers aid in conducting the course? _____ _____

35 Are there films, videotapes, slides and overhead transparencies available on the subject? _____ _____

ASSESSING THE LEARNING STYLES OF PARTICIPANTS AND INSTRUCTORS

Step 3 of the course design procedure is determining what the learning style preferences of course personnel are. It is important to have some understanding of how participants are likely to behave towards each other and how participants 'process' new information in their heads. Interactive style is the pattern of a person's behaviour and preferences to behave in certain ways in relation to other people. Cognitive style is the pattern of a person's characteristic way of thinking about new information and experiences. Together these two styles help us to predict how the person will probably act during the course and what preferences he or she will have about being treated by the staff.

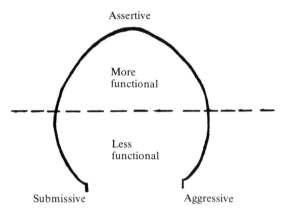

Figure 4.2

Interactive style, or interpersonal behaviour pattern can be specified in many ways. We have chosen to focus on a horseshoe-shaped continuum of assertiveness as shown in Figure 4.2. This model, developed by Kelley (1979), indicates that both submissive and aggressive behaviours can be problematic. Adopting an assertive style or interacting with others gets one's needs met while respecting the rights of others.

Cognitive style, or usual patterns of ways of thinking about new information and experiences can also be treated in many ways. We have elected to represent it in terms that are receiving increasing support in research on brain functioning. The three broad thinking patterns have been labelled rational, holistic, and intuitive. They

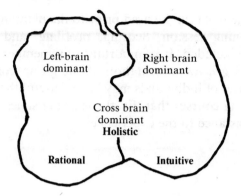

Figure 4.3

can be depicted as shown in Figure 4.3. Of course, this model is
a gross oversimplification of how the brain works, but it is commonly
observed that scientific and technical managers tend to think ration-
ally and that many female managers are highly intuitive.

Together these two models indicate important things about how
people prefer to learn. The matrix in Figure 4.4 integrates these two

Interactive style Cognitive style	Submissive	Assertive	Aggressive
Rational	Seeing	Problem solving	Investigating
Holistic	Being	Processing	Bridging
Intuitive	Flowing	Creating	Committing

Figure 4.4

aspects of personality. The gerunds in the nine cells represent the
most likely behaviour of people who have that dominant interactive
style and that dominant cognitive style. A person who is aggressive
in interacting with other persons and who is essentially rational in
his or her thinking is likely to challenge the instructor and ask a lot
of questions.

The learning style assessment inventory is designed to survey course
participants and instructors regarding their preferred ways of behaving in relation to each other and of taking in new information and

experiences. The scale can be used prior to the planning of the course or in the opening session. Scoring, profiling, and interpretation suggestions are included. It is important to remember that this questionnaire yields *general* information about group composition and that the responses of individuals may be less useful than broad group trends. Designing courses that 'fit' the learning styles of participants can obviate resistance to the experience.

LEARNING STYLE ASSESSMENT

Name

Date

This inventory explores your preferred ways of learning. You will be asked to rate the degree to which a number of statements are true to you. Use the letters in the following scale to indicate your response to each item:

SA Strongly agree
A   Agree
U   Uncertain or undecided
D   Disagree
SD Strongly disagree

Remember that there are no right or wrong answers to the answers; what is 'right' is what is descriptive of you. Do not leave any items blank.

This assessment will be helpful in determining how your training and development experiences will be designed and conducted. You will receive feedback on your preferred style of learning.

1   It is important for me to develop an understanding of the theory being presented.
2   I look for ways to apply what I learn to problems I am facing in my work.
3   In the training room I tend to challenge and question the instructor.
4   It is characteristic of me to adopt the attitude, 'let it be'.
5   I tend to try to find new ways of integrating what I am learning with what I already know, to achieve a kind of synergy, or new reality.
6   I attempt actively to organise what I am learning into systems that make sense to me.
7   In a learning situation I usually 'go with the flow'.
8   When I am in the process of learning I go beyond the data to create new ideas.
9   My learning works best when I think of ways of changing my behaviour to incorporate new information.

10   I look for the important features to be presented to me by the instructor.

11   My preference is for material to be presented in a highly practical way.

12   I like a good 'free-for-all' discussion in which people's ideas are attacked openly.

13   The instructor can expect me to accept his or her major premises willingly.

14   I look for ideas and methods that get me beyond my 'yes, but' reactions.

15   New information triggers in me an attempt at bridging between theory and practicality.

16   In training and development courses I tend to go along with the programme co-operatively.

17   While I am learning something my mind creates new ideas and applications.

18   I learn best when I feel committed to doing something active with the new information and skills.

19   My initial reaction to being taught is to try to understand the material thoroughly.

20   I prefer to learn through applying new information in problem-solving exercises.

21   I tend to feel argumentative when I am listening to a training presentation.

22   Trainers would probably describe me as 'just being there'.

23   I take active responsibility for relating my thoughts and feelings.

24   In learning new material I work best when I find my own way to organise it.

25   My learning style could be described as sponge-like – I tend simply to soak up new information.

26   I am stimulated by new ideas to find new applications.

27   I am likely to remember new information because I commit myself to trying it out in the 'real world'.

28   It pleases me to apprehend clearly what the instructor is saying.

29   I like case studies in training because I get to work out practical solutions.

30   In my opinion, a sceptical attitude is best for reacting to new information.

31 I feel most comfortable in training situations when the instructor does not put me 'on the spot'.
32 When I am learning new material, I find myself reflecting a lot on my experience.
33 The instructor should clearly show connections between his or her materials and my work.
34 It is easy for me to submit myself to what the instructor asks me to do.
35 I am most creative when I am engaged in learning something.
36 I am willing to take risks in applying what I learn.
37 When I am on a training course, I like it when the instructor 'makes the lights go on' in my head.
38 I enjoy trying to figure things out while I am learning new information.
39 My instinctive response to lecture material is to argue with it.
40 I appreciate new information because it enlarges my enjoyment of just being in the world.
41 When new data seem contradictory to what I think I already know, I seek to develop a different reality for myself.
42 I am the type of person who organises new information into my own categories.
43 On training courses I tend to be submissive, giving the leadership to the instructor.
44 Learning is exciting and satisfying for me when I am engaged in creative activities.
45 I am not afraid to argue with others in the training group when I disagree with their ideas.
46 When the presentation seems reasonable, I tend to be receptive to the material.
47 I need to see how new information will help me to face the problems I have in my work.
48 On training courses I tend to be one of the participants who ask a lot of questions.
49 I like it when the instructor is informing me in ways that are sensitive to my feelings.
50 I learn best through discussions of my own and others' experiences.
51 When I encounter new ways of thinking and doing, I tend

to look for systematic ways of linking them to what I already know.

52 When the course participants get along well together, I feel most open to learning.

53 I like to participate in training exercises that require the group to be creative.

54 On training courses I like the instructor to push me and others into making commitments.

55 I prefer to be told by the instructor what has to be found to be useful.

56 I derive more from learning when I have worked out my own practical solutions.

57 I act aggressively when I am being exposed to material that I find to be unreasonable.

58 My basic style in participating in training courses is to take the whole experience somewhat submissively.

59 I take an active role in looking for ways to integrate my work experience with new information.

60 For me, acquiring new information and skills means pushing forward to a higher level of organisation within myself.

61 As a learner I could be described as both submissive and intuitive.

62 I feel most excited in training courses when I am challenged to brainstorm and create.

63 In training groups I am usually seen as a risk-taker.

64 I like the instructor to point out the rationale of his or her material so that I can develop a complete understanding.

65 I am most receptive to training when I am led to apply new information to actual problems I face on the job.

66 I react negatively to instructors who place a lot of emphasis on feelings.

67 When I get the material being presented into perspective, I tend to accept it.

68 I enjoy participative activities in training courses such as role playing, taking inventories and team discussions.

69 When I am being given new models and theories I aggressively attempt to relate them to mine and others' experiences.

70 I pay attention to my intuitive reactions as to what the instructor is giving me.

71 My response to new theories and methods is to adapt them to my own ways of thinking and behaving.

72 I am ready and willing to 'stick my neck out' in training courses to get people to listen to what I believe is useful and true.

SCORING THE LEARNING STYLE ASSESSMENT INVENTORY

Instructions

Go back through the questionnaire and assign numbers to the letters you wrote in front of the items. Use the following scale:

$$SA = 4 \ A = 3 \ U = 2 \ D = 1 \ SD = 0$$

Then copy the numerical ratings into the appropriate spaces below and add them within each category

Item rating	*Item rating*	*Item rating*
1 _____	2 _____	3 _____
10 _____	11 _____	12 _____
19 _____	20 _____	21 _____
28 _____	29 _____	30 _____
37 _____	38 _____	39 _____
46 _____	47 _____	48 _____
55 _____	56 _____	57 _____
64 _____	65 _____	66 _____
Sum A [ ]	Sum B [ ]	Sum C [ ]

Item rating	*Item rating*	*Item rating*
4 _____	5 _____	6 _____
13 _____	14 _____	15 _____
22 _____	23 _____	24 _____
31 _____	32 _____	33 _____
40 _____	41 _____	42 _____
49 _____	50 _____	51 _____
58 _____	59 _____	60 _____
67 _____	68 _____	69 _____
Sum D [ ]	Sum E [ ]	Sum F [ ]

Item rating	*Item rating*	*Item rating*
7 _____	8 _____	9 _____
16 _____	17 _____	18 _____
25 _____	26 _____	27 _____
34 _____	35 _____	36 _____
43 _____	44 _____	45 _____
52 _____	53 _____	54 _____
61 _____	62 _____	63 _____
70 _____	71 _____	72 _____
Sum G [ ]	Sum H [ ]	Sum I [ ]

You will transfer these sums to the learning style assessment profile sheet.

LEARNING STYLE ASSESSMENT PROFILE SHEET

Instructions

Transfer your sums from the scoresheet into the matrix below. Then add the columns and rows.

Style in acquiring information \ Interacting style	Submissive	Assertive	Aggressive	Overall style in acquiring information
Rational	*Seeing* Understanding [A]	*Problem Solving* Pragmatic [B]	*Investigating* Challenging Questioning [C]	[ ] Rational
Holistic	*Being* 'letting it be' [D]	*Processing* Toward Synergy [E]	*Bridging* Linking Organising [F]	[ ] Holistic
Intuitive	*Flowing* 'Going with the flow' [G]	*Creating* Going beyond the data [H]	*Committing* Willing Risking [I]	[ ] Intuitive
Overall style in interacting	[ ] Submissiveness	[ ] Assertiveness	[ ] Aggressiveness	[ ] Flexibility

97

As you can see from the matrix there are nine cells indicating the approaches to learning. Your highest scores represent your preferences for how to learn in training and development courses. You may have a dominant style in acquiring information (cognitive tendency) and one for interacting with the instructor and other participants (interpersonal orientation). The two aspects of learning style are reflected in the nine cells of the matrix. The highest scores inside the matrix indicate your preferred ways of learning, and your lowest scores show how you are likely to find learning to be satisfactory.

Of course, you can choose to change your preferences by experimenting with your behaviour and by consciously engaging in thinking about information in new ways. You can take the occasion of the course to attempt to bolster those styles that are least likely for you. If you ordinarily act aggressively, for example, you may deliberately act more assertively or even become submissive for a while. If you ordinarily are rational, linear and cause-and-effect in your thinking (left brain dominant), you may stretch yourself into paying attention to your hunches and 'gut reactions' and visualising (right brain dominant). In other words, you can increase your flexibility in participating in training and development courses through purposeful attempts at behaving and thinking differently.

PLANNING LEARNING ACTIVITIES FOR ADULTS

In the course design procedure outlined earlier in this chapter step 5 is reflecting on adult-learning principles and their implications for planning learning activities. It is important to remember that adults are not children. Managers expect to be treated as responsible adults when they attend development courses. Before designing the course the instructor should set aside a period of reflection to be reminded of basic principles of adult learning and their design implications. The accompanying chart lists sixteen principles to be considered, along with design principles for each. The management development staff might profitably discuss these with each other and might also consider publishing them in the opening course session in order to explain the design and hoped-for course norms.

These principles have profound implications for not only designing courses but also carrying out the designs. In the next chapter, on facilitator style, we shall discuss the implications of this way of thinking about management development in choosing one's instructional role. Here we want to suggest strongly that each principle be studied before planning course structure and activities.

PRINCIPLES OF ADULT LEARNING AND COURSE DESIGN

Learning principles	Implications for course design
The adult is a partner with the instructor in the learning process	Participants should actively influence the learning approach
Adults are capable of taking responsibility for their own learning	Incorporate self-directed learning activities in the course design
Adult learners gain through two-way communication	Avoid over-use of lectures and 'talking-to', emphasise discussion
Adults learn through reflection on their and others' experience	Use interactive methods such as case studies, role-playing, etc.
Adults learn what they perceive to be useful in their life situations	Make the content and materials closely fit assessed needs
Adults' attention spans are a function of their interest in the experience	Allow plenty of time to 'process' the learning activities
Adults are most receptive to instruction that is clearly related to problems they face daily	Include applications planning in each learning activity
Adults learn best when they are being treated with respect	Promote giving inquiry into problems and affirm the experience of participants
Adults do not typically see themselves as learners	Give participants a rationale for becoming involved and provide opportunities for success
Adults learn better in a climate that is informal and personal	Promote getting acquainted and interpersonal linkages

Learning principles	Implications for course design
Adult learners apply learning that they have been influential in planning	Diagnose and prioritise learning needs and preferences during the course as well as before
Adults learn when they feel supported in experimenting with new ideas and skills	Use learning groups as 'home bases' for participants
Adults are likely to have somewhat fixed points of view that make them closed to new ways of thinking and behaving	Include interpersonal feedback exercises and opportunities to experiment
Adults learn to react to the differential status of members of the group	Use sub-groups to provide safety and readiness to engage in open interchange
Adults are internally motivated to develop increased effectiveness	Make all learner evaluation self-directed
Adults filter their learning through their values systems	Provide activities that focus on cognitive, affective and behavioural change

SELECTING APPROPRIATE TRAINING TECHNOLOGIES

In general, trainers talk too much, they overuse the lecture method. While that approach is useful to impart concepts and develop perspective, it is almost totally inappropriate for developing skills and changing attitudes. Consequently, we propose in step 6 of the course design procedure that the instructional staff select appropriate technologies for achieving each course objective. In most cases this will result in using multiple methods throughout the course.

In general, there are three categories of training technologies. One includes methods that are designed to introduce concepts and information and to develop a sense of perspective on content. The second includes techniques for developing skills. The third focuses more on learning about oneself. Each of the categories has a different set of assumptions about how people learn underpinning it.

Category One: Didactic

This set of technologies is primarily used for introducing new information and for helping participants to recognise the important features. This is the category that is most used for cognitive objectives, and it is the most abused approach. It includes reading, lecturing, experiential lecturing (lectures broken up by brief interactive exercises), tape/slide presentations, movie/videotape presentations, and many forms of programmed learning. The basic learning theory here is people learn information through hearing and seeing it and being shown its interconnectedness. The difficulties with this approach are that it is often experienced as dull and boring and that it is ineffective in promoting ownership and responsibility taking on the part of course participants.

Category Two: Skill-building exercises

This set of technologies is intended to generate increased effectiveness in the behaviour of participants. It includes group discussion, skill exercises, case studies, role-plays, and problem-solving activities. Group discussion is in the area between categories one and two, in that it can be used to help consolidate understanding of material that has been presented didactically and also for developing skills in human interaction. Our formula for effective group discussion has five steps:

1 Prepare participants for group discussion. They may be instructed to make notes to themselves beforehand.
2 Give the group a task to perform. The task should involve skills that they already have and new ones they are developing. The discussion then becomes essential to accomplish the task. Many managers are more highly task-oriented than interaction-oriented, and couching discussion in terms of tasks appeals to them.
3 Have the group create a product. This can be a list, statement, chart, graphic presentation or object.
4 Have the group present its product to other groups. This creates a situation of mild competitiveness that can motivate the group to do the task thoroughly.
5 Reinforce group productivity. This can be simply verbal recognition or applause.

This category of training technologies has a different theoretical rationale from category one. Skill building is basically and fundamentally different from learning concepts. A skill is any human behaviour that can be done better. That is, there is a prior consideration of quality and a plan to develop behaviour that approximates to an ideal. For example, braking a car is a skill; understanding how brakes work is not. The general learning theory for skill acquisition is behavioural. It says that people become more effective when they succeed in matching behaviours that have been deemed desirable. The theory can be described in a series of steps:

1 Present a model of how the effective behaviour looks;
2 Provide opportunities to practise behaviours toward the model;
3 Provide learners with knowledge of their results (feedback);
4 Reinforce behaviours that show progress toward the ideal.

These technologies involve 'shaping' behaviour towards externally established criteria of effectiveness.

Category Three: Inductive learning

Whereas category one approaches emphasise deductive thinking ('If this is true, then'), the more highly experiential methods in

category three stress learning through discovery. Generalisations
are developed as a result of the experience that participants share
during the course activities. These technologies include self assessment instruments such as those included in this book, structured
experiences, simulation games, interpersonal feedback exchanges,
personal goal-setting designs and unstructured group interactions
(T-groups, encounter, etc.). The rationale in this category is different
from both of the previous two. All of these technologies involve
doing things and then talking about them to abstract learning. The
basic theory is captured in the Experiential Learning Cycle (Pfeiffer
& Jones, 1981); see Figure 4.5. This theory and approach to learning
emphasises active involvement of participants in interactions that
are discussed ('processed') for the purpose of discovering what
works.

The training technology analysis worksheet presents these three
categories of technologies opposite the objectives of the course being
designed. In general, cognitive objectives are best achieved by using
methods found in categories one and three; affective ones call for

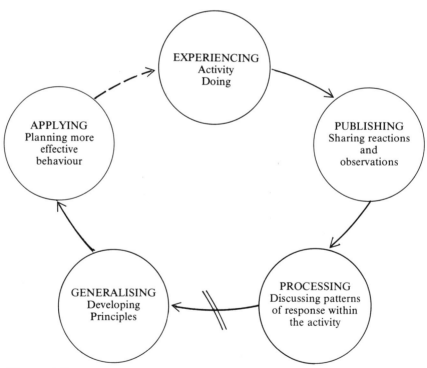

Figure 4.5

category three methods, and behavioural goals are best approached by category two technologies. At this point we are not designing the course itself, but we are simply selecting the training technologies that will be incorporated into the design later. Notice that the technologies included on the training technology analysis worksheet have been arranged on a loose continuum of involvement. On the top of the list, in category one, are methods that feature low learner involvement, and the ones in category three, towards the bottom, require learners to be actively involved. In general, the more actively involved managers are in the learning process the more likely they are to 'own' the outcomes and apply their knowledge back on the job. This is not to imply that any category of technologies is 'better' than the other two. All three must usually be represented in designs of effective courses.

TRAINING TECHNOLOGIES ANALYSIS

Instructions

Use this form to plan the methods to be used in the course being designed. Across the top of the chart write brief statements of essential course objectives. Then for each objective select the appropriate techniques by writing your planning ideas (names of activities, resources, development needs etc.) in the column.

Course Objectives Established by Needs Assessment / Training Technology	Highest Priority Objective	Objective 2	Objective 3	Objective 4
Reading				
Lecture				
Experiential Lecture				
Tape-slide Presentation				
Movie/ Video-tape				
Programmed Learning				

Category One: Didactic

Category Two: Skill Building	Group Discussion
	Skill Exercise
	Case Study
	Role Play
	Problem Solving
Category Three: Discovery	Self-Assessment Instrument
	Structured Experience
	Simulation
	Interpersonal Feedback
	Personal Goal-Setting
	Unstructured Group Interaction

DESIGNING THE OPENING AND CLOSING SESSIONS

The first and last sessions of any management development course are the most important. The first sets the tone for the entire experience, and the last hopefully leads to managers going away to apply their learnings confidently. Consequently, it is crucial to plan these sessions first and in some detail.

The opening session is vitally important to get things going in a positive way. It is exceedingly difficult to recover from a bad beginning in a management development course. Consequently, we offer the following general considerations for designing the first meeting of the course.

Initial contact	Plan the introductory comments to be brief; present them *visually* as well as auditorially
Ice breaking	Include some interactive activity that will get participants speaking with each other easily
Checking expectations	Involve participants in diagnosing what they want and don't want in the course
Overview	Present the course GORONOVAD
	Goals – responsibilities of instructor/ participants
	Roles – expectations of participants and of instructors
	Norms – push sensitivity, participation, experimentation, responsibility and openness (SPERO)
	Overview – a broad outline of the organisation of the course
	Administration – announcements about messages, meals, resources etc.
Goal setting	Involve participants in specifying what they want to emphasise in their learning
Integrative theory	Present a macro-model that shows the interrelationship of the course content/ skill areas
Team development	Establish learning groups and have them develop team identities (name, logo, motto, cheer) to be presented to the entire group

Volunteering	Have each team select representatives to committees: refreshments, morale, evaluation, recreation, housekeeping, equipment, banquet, talent show follow-through etc.
Bridging	Make team reading assignments and present an outline of the next session
Closing	Give the clear expectation that what comes next will be interesting, stimulating, involving and useful

The final course session must be thought through carefully at the beginning. The designers ask 'In what stage do I want participants when they walk out of the door at the end?' The following general considerations can be helpful in designing the end of the course.

Premature closure	Give the clear expectation that this session will be a most important and a most useful one; challenge people not to 'switch off' until later
Leftovers	Respond to all leftover topics and questions.
Strength bombardment	Centre on the positive characteristics of each participant. For example, teams create awards for all individuals in the other teams.
Final applications planning	Design activities for individuals to prioritise their applications commitments and to share them with each other
Learning group closure	Have small-group members 'finish' their group's business
Planning follow-through	Establish network procedures, follow-up contacts and sessions
Group statements	Invite statements of appreciation to the entire group
Last minute connections	Permit individuals to signal their interest in seeing each other just after the session

Evaluation

Solicit end-of-course evaluative data and suggestions

Closure

Send people out on a note of positive expectation

DESIGN SUPPORT MATERIALS

The following publications contain numerous training models and technologies that can be used in designing management development courses.

Francis, D. and Woodcock, M., *Unblocking Your Organisation,* San Diego, CA: University Associates 1979.

Pfeiffer, J. W. and Jones, J. E. eds, *A Handbook of Structured Experiences for Human Relations Training* (vol. 8), San Diego, CA; University Associates, 1981.

Pfeiffer, J. W. and Jones, J. E. eds, *The Annual Handbook for Group Facilitators,* San Diego, CA: University Associates, 1972–82.

Pfeiffer, J. W. and Jones, J. E. eds, *The Structured Experience Kit,* San Diego, CA: University Associates, 1981.

Pfeiffer, J. W., Heslin, R. and Jones, J. E., *Instrumentation in Human Relations Training,* San Diego, CA: University Associates, 1976.

Woodcock, M. and Francis, D., *The Unblocked Manager,* Aldershot, Hampshire: Gower 1982.

REFERENCES

Ingalls, J. D., *Human Energy: The Critical Factor for Individuals and Organizations.* Austin, TX: Learning Concepts, 1979.

Kelley, C. K., *Assertion Training: A Facilitator's Guide.* San Diego, CA: University Associates, 1979.

Knowles, M. S., *The Modern Practice of Adult Education: Andragogy vs Pedagogy.* NY: Association Press, 1970.

Pfeiffer, J. W. and Jones, J. E., *Reference Guide to the Handbooks and Annuals.* San Diego, CA: University Associates, 1981.

Pfeiffer, J. W. and Jones, J. E., 'Design Considerations in Laboratory Education'. In J. E. Jones and J. W. Pfeiffer (eds) *The 1973 Annual Handbook for Group Facilitators.* San Diego, CA: University Associates, 1973.

5 Developing an effective training style

In the previous chapter we used the idea of a three-legged stool to show the interdependence of course content, design, and trainer style. In this section we will expand our understanding of what constitutes an effective training style. The goal in this chapter is to help management development professionals to assess various aspects of their overall styles and to establish priorities for improving their ability to deliver results–producing courses.

The role of the trainer/facilitator/instructor needs to be clarified and what determines how effectively he or she carries out the role needs to be studied. Firstly, it is our observation that there are six crucial dimensions that impinge upon trainer role effectiveness. Although the model shown in Figure 5.1 depicts these six facets of trainer competency separately, in reality they probably overlap significantly. In other words, for the person to carry out a training role successfully, he or she needs to know the subject, know training methods, be able to relate to adults effectively, know how to use experiential methods in designing courses, be skilful in working with group dynamics, and have an appropriate personal/professional manner.

We have been using the terms trainer, facilitator, and instructor interchangeably in this book because that is common practice in the management development field. It is useful for style purposes, however, to make some distinctions among these roles and others. The chart on p. 113 outlines what we believe to be the chief differences among roles that people take when attempting to help others develop. It can be seen that a course that uses all three categories of training

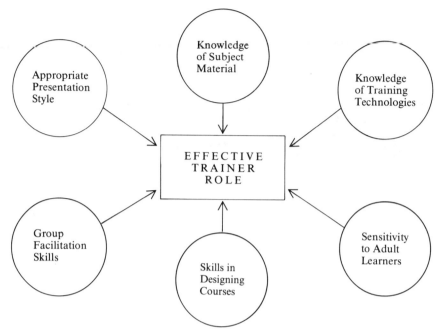

Figure 5.1

technologies discussed in the last chapter would require that the person in charge plays multiple roles. Part of the time he or she would be facilitating, training, teaching, instructing and even perhaps counselling and consulting. We believe that it is necessary for management development professionals to have sufficient role flexibility so as to work towards the kind of desired outcomes included in the last column of the chart.

SUBJECT MATTER COMPETENCY

When managers talk about trainers that they like, they often point out that good ones 'know their subject'. We believe that it is impossible to fake knowledge about management to trainees. We are probably much more transparent in this area than in any other aspect of trainer effectiveness. When we are cognitively prepared, we exude an air of confidence into the course room, and our presentation job is easier. We become more able to pay attention to other things, such as group maintenance.

The subject matter competency analysis questionnaire is intended

SOME CONTRASTS AMONG DEVELOPMENTAL ROLES

DIMENSION / ROLE	'HELPEES'	ROLE VIS-A-VIS 'HELPEES'	CONTENT EMPHASIS	LOCUS OF MEANING	DESIRED OUTCOMES
FACILITATOR	Participants	Helper in a Discovery Process	Inductive Learning	Individual 'Helpees'	Discovery and Application
TRAINER	Trainees	Shaper of Effective Behaviour	Skill Acquisition	In the Trainer	Effective Behaviour
INSTRUCTOR (TECHNICAL TRAINING)	Students	Expert and a Demonstrator	'How to . . .'	In Definition of Effectiveness	Strategy, Tactic, and Technique
TEACHER	Students	Imparter of Information & Meaning	Conceptual Understanding	In the Teacher's Interpretation	Awareness and Understanding
COUNSELLOR	Clients/ Counselees	Permissive Helper	Client Life Situations and Feelings	In the Individual Client	'Wise Choices'
CONSULTANT	Clients	Helper in Problem Solving	Client Situations That Need Attention	In the Client System	Responsibility in Implementing Solution to Problem Situations

to provide a self-check on how well the training staff is prepared in the content areas covered by the course. This version of the questionnaire is built around the managerial competencies model presented in Chapter 2. Any given management development course may not be concerned with these twenty content areas, and the form must be adapted in each case. Technical subjects, such as finance and law, are not included because our model deals exclusively with the human aspects of management. This questionnaire can provide an agenda for trainers to prepare themselves to run management development courses.

SUBJECT MATTER COMPETENCY ANALYSIS

Instructions

This inventory is designed to assist you in determining your readiness in the various subject matter areas of the managerial competencies model. This is not an assessment of your skills but of your preparedness in *content*. Rate yourself on each of the subject matter areas. Then develop a learning agenda for yourself in the areas in which you do not feel confident.

	I need to study this content area before attempting to present it	I generally know this content, but I need to review it before presentation	I understand this material well enough to explain it to managers right away

Managing self

1	Managing theory	____	____	____
2	Values	____	____	____
3	Self-management	____	____	____
4	Communication	____	____	____
5	Goal setting	____	____	____
6	Decision making	____	____	____
7	Problem solving	____	____	____
8	Conflict management	____	____	____

Managing subordinates

9	Leadership style	____	____	____
10	Team development	____	____	____
11	Performance review	____	____	____
12	Coaching and counselling	____	____	____

Managing organisational interfaces

13 Managing
    organisational
    behaviour   _____   _____   _____
14 Managing inter-team
    relations   _____   _____   _____
15 Conducting effective
    meetings   _____   _____   _____
16 Managing change   _____   _____   _____
17 Project management   _____   _____   _____

Managing external relations

18 Managing public
    relations   _____   _____   _____
19 Managing customer/
    client/supplier
    relations   _____   _____   _____
20 Recruitment and
    orientation   _____   _____   _____

IMPROVING PRESENTATION SKILLS

In this section we focus on that part of trainer effectiveness represented by making good presentations in front of groups. A trainer may know the subject, but if he or she cannot deliver it well to groups of managers, the outcomes of the course are jeopardised. Remember that a skill is any behaviour that can be done better. The presentation skills inventory contains the vitai 'be-able-to-do-well' skill areas that we have found to be important in making management development courses work. The staff must be able to communicate, use audiovisual supports, work with the group in ways that keep it functioning well, and help participants learn through good 'processing'.

This inventory enables the trainer to take stock of his or her skills level and to develop priorities for improvement. Conducting management development courses gives us many opportunities to work on our skills. For example, both of the authors of this book have to fight a tendency to talk too much in training situations, and we often ask the group's help in changing that behaviour.

This questionnaire was developed after the general format of an inventory on consulting skills (Pfeiffer and Jones, 1976). Trainers who are consultants may also wish to study the consulting skills inventory.

PRESENTATION SKILLS INVENTORY

Instructions

This questionnaire is designed to help you assess your skills in various aspects of making presentations to training groups. As a result of this inventory you will have a more comprehensive understanding of your strengths as a presenter as well as your learning priorities for improving yourself as a group facilitator.

Go over the list of skills *twice*. First, mark each skill area according to whether you're OK on it or need to improve. Then go back over the skills for which you perceive a need to improve and circle the item numbers of *three or four* that you wish to emphasise at this time for your own development.

		OK	Need to improve
Communication			
1	Listening		
2	Expressing myself clearly		
3	Being brief and concise		
4	Building on the ideas of others		
5	Talking to participants		
6	Helping participants understand		
7	Asking questions		
8	Answering questions		
9	Giving examples or illustrations		
10	Using appropriate gestures		
11	Modulating my voice		
12	Giving directions and instructions		
13	Translating technical terminology into everyday speech		
14	Avoiding unnecessary jargon		
15	Using humour		
16	Using anecdotes		
17	Adapting my language to participants' cognitive styles		
18	Other		

	OK	Need to improve

Audiovisual aids

		OK	Need to improve
19	Preparing attractive, clear posters		
20	Posting participant comments and data		
21	Using slides and overhead transparencies		
22	Introducing movies and videotapes		
23	Facilitating discussions of audiovisual presentations		
24	Other		

Group maintenance

		OK	Need to improve
25	Sensing the feeling level of the group		
26	Using energisers to 'pep up' the presentation		
27	Modulating the intensity of the event		
28	Showing enthusiasm		
29	'Checking the temperature' of the group		
30	Modifying my presentation spontaneously		
31	Observing group process		
32	Handling difficult participants		
33	Negotiating design and schedule changes with participants		
34	Holding the interest of the group		
35	Facilitating interpersonal feedback sessions		
36	Other		

Processing

		OK	Need to improve
37	Drawing out learnings from participants		
38	Using open-ended questions		
39	Finding themes in the outcomes of experiential activities		
40	Adding my experience to that of participants		
41	Helping participants plan applications of their learnings		
42	Other		

PROFILING THE TRAINER'S STYLE

Trainers differ widely in their manner of making presentations and relating to participants. Some apparently think that they have to project an image of seriousness, and others resemble entertainers. Sales trainers, for example, often have to show considerable enthusiasm and actually 'sell' their subject. Our beliefs in this area are clear. We believe that professionals who conduct courses in which managers participate should be high profile models of what they are 'teaching'.

The facilitator style profile rating sheet was developed from discussions and observations about what constitutes an effective training style. It represents what we should and ought to do and also their opposites. The twenty-six dimensions together describe how we think a trainer should be in a management development course. As a good Boy Scout should be 'trustworthy, loyal, helpful, courteous, etc.', a good trainer should be 'supportive, participating, talking with, etc.'. Of course, all trainers would not be expected to agree, since it is more important to be yourself than it is to play-act. We are proposing an ideal.

The profile sheet can be used for feedback as well as self assessment. The training staff may wish to ask course participants to fill in the ratings by placing the initials of the staff on each line instead of Xs. This practice can open the course as a learning system and can legitimise confronting the trainer. It can also, of course, provide consensual validation for one's self ratings.

FACILITATOR STYLE PROFILE

Instructions

Think of your *manner* of presentation in front of training groups – how you deliver information, set up activities and relate to participants. On each of the twenty-six bi-polar scales below write an 'X' to indicate your usual presentation manner. Be honest with yourself. Then go back and circle those adjectives that describe how you would like to improve. This will help you to develop an agenda for your professional development as a group facilitator.

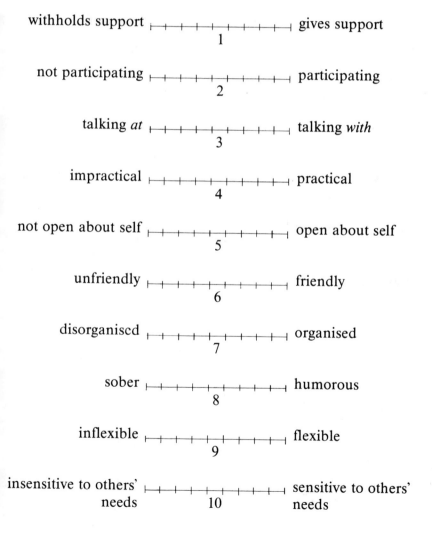

withholds support   1   gives support

not participating   2   participating

talking *at*   3   talking *with*

impractical   4   practical

not open about self   5   open about self

unfriendly   6   friendly

disorganised   7   organised

sober   8   humorous

inflexible   9   flexible

insensitive to others' needs   10   sensitive to others' needs

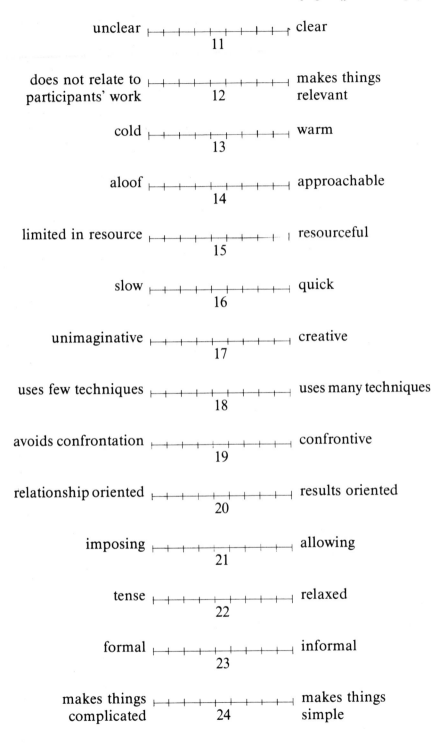

unclear ———————— clear
11

does not relate to ———————— makes things
participants' work   12   relevant

cold ———————— warm
13

aloof ———————— approachable
14

limited in resource ———————— resourceful
15

slow ———————— quick
16

unimaginative ———————— creative
17

uses few techniques ———————— uses many techniques
18

avoids confrontation ———————— confrontive
19

relationship oriented ———————— results oriented
20

imposing ———————— allowing
21

tense ———————— relaxed
22

formal ———————— informal
23

makes things ———————— makes things
complicated   24   simple

serious ├──┼──┼──┼──┼──┼──┼──┤ playful
25

playing safe ├──┼──┼──┼──┼──┼──┼──┤ taking risks
26

STYLE IN HANDLING CRITICAL INCIDENTS

Sometimes things occur in management development courses that require the trainer to respond. We call these occurrences 'critical incidents' because we believe that they compel the trainer to be careful in reacting. Some events disrupt the course climate, and others threaten the maintenance of an effective group community. Cohen and Smith (1976) outlined methods for dealing with these types of happenings in personal-growth groups. Here we are concerned with assessing the trainer's style in handling difficult situations and with managing one's style to be maximally responsive to the needs of participants and the requirements of the course.

The critical training incidents inventory was based on an earlier instrument developed by Jones and Banet (1978). It contains fifteen things that happen from time to time in management development courses. It is our contention that trainers should be prepared for all contingencies, and we have selected representative ones for inclusion in the scale. This is a good inventory for getting acquainted with one's co-facilitator, since staff styles might profitably be complementary. A good way of improving one's readiness to deal with these incidents is to study Jones' (1979) paper on 'Dealing with Disruptive Individuals in Meetings'. It is written for managers, but trainers can easily adapt its methods.

CRITICAL TRAINING INCIDENTS INVENTORY

Instructions

This questionnaire is designed to help you to assess your style in handling difficult group situations. Each of the items presents a critical incident that requires the facilitator to respond in some way. There are three alternatives to consider in each case. Distribute five points among the three options according to what you would probably do (not necessarily what you *should* do) in the situation. For example, if you would most likely do A, a little bit of B, and no C, your point distribution might be 4–1–0. Make sure your points add up to 5 for each item. Do not omit any items.

1   You are introducing a structured experience when a participant interrupts and says that the activity is irrelevant. You say,
  A   I understand how you might feel that way. ☐
  B   Listen again to the goals of this exercise. ☐
  C   Let's see what others think about doing it. ☐

2   About two-thirds into a lecture you overhear a participant say to another, in a stage whisper, 'This is a load of bull!'. You . . .
  A   Let the incident go unnoticed for fear of embarrassing the participant. ☐
  B   Confront the person's sabotage of another's learning. ☐
  C   Ask how you might make the presentation more useful. ☐

3   In the second session of the course you notice that subgroups are sticking together – levels of management, minorities, men and women, etc. You . . .
  A   Plan in activities to bring the members of these groups closer together. ☐
  B   You point out your concerns and suggest that they mix with each other more. ☐
  C   You conduct a diagnostic activity to determine how people want to relate to each other. ☐

4   You are making several serious points in your presentation, but two participants are 'horsing around' with each other in a disruptive manner. You . . .
  A   Ask politely if they would rather do something else. ☐
  B   Firmly suggest that they are being disruptive and ask them to pay attention. ☐

C   Stop the presentation and assess the preferences of the
group for continuing.   ☐

5   You notice that two or three participants always tend to come to
the sessions a bit late. You ...
A   Acknowledge that they are very busy managers.   ☐
B   Indicate strongly that you expect punctuality and
intend to begin without them.   ☐
C   Facilitate a problem-identification/problem-solving
exchange on the schedule.   ☐

6   A participant makes an outright refusal to fill out a self-assessment instrument on his or her leadership style. You say,
A   I understand that you don't see the usefulness of this
activity.   ☐
B   I think that you will profit from completing this. If you
don't see it that way, please don't spoil the experience
for others.   ☐
C   What would be a better way for you to study how you
influence others who work for you?   ☐

7   A participant comes to the session either inebriated or 'high' on
some drug. He or she is largely incapable of participating
effectively in the meeting. You ...
A   Take the person aside and gently offer the option of
non-attendance at the session.   ☐
B   Ask the person either to be quiet and observe or leave
the session.   ☐
C   Open up the situation as a group problem and facilitate
the discussion.   ☐

8   You are introducing an interpersonal feedback exercise, and
you notice that the non-verbal 'body language' of several
participants seems to indicate fear. You ...
A   Reassure people that no one will get hurt in the activity. ☐
B   Give participants instructions on how to manage their
feedback and feelings during the exercise.   ☐
C   Ask the group to help you to redesign the activity so as
to minimise the threat.   ☐

9   After a competitive exercise the group is discussing learnings,
and one participant begins to cry. You ...
A   Quietly ask the person to leave with you for a few
moments while the group continues.   ☐

B   Stop the discussion and ask participants to extend their
     understanding and support to the person.   ☐
C   Point out that this is happening and ask the group what
     it wants to do about it.   ☐

10 You ask the group for data, and no one responds (a dead
    response). You say . . .
    A   I can understand that you may have nothing to say at
        this point.   ☐
    B   Let's try it this way: take out a piece of paper and write
        down for me . . .   ☐
    C   What would be a good way for us to proceed now?   ☐

11 During the first sessions of the course one person has established
    a pattern of dominating group discussion. The participant cuts
    off others to make his or her point repeatedly. You . . .
    A   Acknowledge that he or she has strong feelings about
        the subject.   ☐
    B   Ask the person to stop interrupting others while you
        solicit their participation.   ☐
    C   Engage the group in analysing its participation patterns
        and making choices about how to modify their dis-
        cussions.   ☐

12 The group begins to attack one member. You . . .
    A   Reassure the 'target' that he or she can change what is
        happening.   ☐
    B   Stop the bombardment and clarify issues and concerns. ☐
    C   Solicit reactions to what is going on and facilitate a
        discussion about how to improve the interaction.   ☐

13 You have conducted a role-play involving manager-subordinate
    conflict, and an unexpectedly high amount of feeling has been
    aroused. There is clearly not enough time in the schedule to
    deal with all of the data that the design has generated. You
    say . . .
    A   We've got a lot of emotional reactions left over from
        what happened in the role-play. Let's share them with
        each other.   ☐
    B   Our time is insufficient to complete this discussion.
        Let's continue, and I will cut back on the next session. ☐
    C   It's clear that we have a lot to say to each other right
        now. Let's decide what we want to do about the
        schedule first.   ☐

14 A member of the participant group makes a sexual overture
    towards you. You ...
    A Are careful not to hurt the other's feelings while you
       refuse.   ☐
    B Point out the 'rules' that govern trainer-participant
       behaviour.   ☐
    C Ask for information on how the two of you might
       continue to work together without spoiling the group's
       experience.   ☐

15 During a coffee break you overhear participants enjoying the
    exchange of racist/sexist humour. You ...
    A Say nothing lest they become embarrassed and see you
       as a spoilsport.   ☐
    B Tell them what your feelings are and request that they
       share different kinds of jokes.   ☐
    C Engage participants in a discussion of creeds within the
       company and what can be done about them.   ☐

CRITICAL TRAINING INCIDENTS SCORING AND INTERPRETATION

Instructions

Check to make certain that your score for each item adds up to 5. Then add the points that you assigned to the alternatives. Add the As for all fifteen items. Do the same for all of the Bs, then the Cs. Write these sums below:

A ☐ Support

B ☐ Direction

C ☐ Problem Solving

The total of these three scores should be 75, since you gave five points to each of the 15 items.

Interpretation

The three behavioural responses that are built into this inventory are support, which is being sensitive to the feelings of participants; direction, which is controlling critical incidents through confrontive leadership; and problem solving, which is assisting the participant group to diagnose and solve the dilemmas in the situation.

Your highest score is your dominant style in dealing with critical incidents in training situations. Your middle score represents your 'back-up' style, or the way you are likely to behave when your dominant style does not work. When your second score is very close to your highest (10 points or less), you may move to your back-up style quickly. Your lowest score represents your least likely behaviour in critical training situations, and it may uncover your 'blind spot'.

MANAGING YOUR STYLE

The effort towards improving one's style should ideally be undertaken in a managed way. That is, the diagnostic instruments in this chapter can be used to determine areas of needed development that can be worked on while actually conducting management development courses. We recommend the following practices are considered in managing the development of trainer style:

1 *Co-train whenever possible.* This enables you to stretch yourself, with professional support. Pfeiffer and Jones (1975) developed a step-by-step procedure for learning in this way.
2 *Set one or two priorities for style change.* Don't attempt to make too many changes in your manner at one time.
3 *Share your style-change objectives with the group.* Participants can give both support and feedback for your improvement.
4 *Let yourself be imperfect.* Since you are trying on new behaviour, do not expect to be good at it right away.
5 *Reward yourself both for trying and for improving.* You know what you are up to, and you need to reinforce your own achievement.
6 *Periodically re-assess all aspects of your style.* Use the instruments in this chapter from time to time to check up on your progress.

Style management means making a committment to working continuously towards high standards of professional behaviour in conducting management development courses. We further believe that one should strive to have the same style in all other management development activities. In the final analysis, effective professionals are the same wherever they are – in the office, at home, in the seminar room.

REFERENCES

Cohen, A. M. and Smith, R. D. *The Critical Incident in Growth Groups,* San Diego, CA: University Associates, 1976.
Jones, J. E. and Banet A. G. Jr. 'The Critical Consulting Incidents Inventory' in Pfeiffer, J. W. and Jones, J. E., eds, *The 1978 Annual Handbook for Group Facilitators,* San Diego, CA: University Associates, 1978.

Jones, J. E. 'Dealing with Disruptive Individuals in Meetings' in Pfeiffer, J. W. and Jones, J. E., eds, *The 1980 Annual Handbook for Group Facilitators,* San Diego, CA: University Associates, 1980.

Pfeiffer, J. W. and Jones, J. E. 'Co-Facilitating' in Jones, J. E. and Pfeiffer, J. W., eds, *The 1975 Annual Handbook for Group Facilitators,* San Diego, CA: University Associates, 1975.

Pfeiffer, J. W. and Jones, J. E., eds, *The 1976 Annual Handbook for Group Facilitators,* San Diego, CA: University Associates, 1976.

6 Logistical planning for management development courses

You have conducted careful training needs assessments, and you have designed what you believe will be a high-impact, useful seminar for managers. Materials have been prepared, and you have scheduled the event to begin tomorrow morning in a hotel conference centre downtown. It is Sunday night, and you arrive at the hotel about 7.00 pm to check in and make final arrangements. You have planned to stay at the hotel during the course since they gave you the use of a bedroom free as a part of the package.

At registration they have no record of your reservation. You had assumed that the sales office of the hotel was going to book your room since they offered it to you. There are several events going on in the building, and the place is fully booked. The events board in the lobby indicates that, among others, a competing organisation is conducting a strategic planning meeting for its executives. You ask for the night manager, who is finally located through her 'walkie-talkie'. She confers with the front desk, and a room is allocated to you. They will, however, have to invoice your company, since they have no record of your booking. They ask to make an imprint of your American Express card. You will have to change rooms tomorrow.

The bedroom is adequate, a little on the small side perhaps, with little or no space for spreading out your materials. You had your materials delivered Friday afternoon to the hotel, and the porter has promised to bring them to your room right away. You unpack your luggage, but there are not enough hangers for your clothes.

You telephone housekeeping, but everyone has left for the night, according to the operator. Your boxes of training materials have not been sent up, so you ring the porter. It becomes clear to you that this person has not located your material, so you urge him to keep trying. Upon inquiring of the front desk about the name of the seminar room you will be using, the person indicates that a banquet is being held there right now and that the room will not be available until sometime after 10.00 p.m. You get instructions for locating the room, which is in an outbuilding. It was your understanding that you would have a seminar room on the mezzanine floor. You telephone the sales office of the hotel, but no one answers.

You decide to have dinner before preparing the training room. They will not seat you in the dining room until you return properly dressed in coat and tie. During dinner you overhear the executives of the competing company discussing their business plans for the coming fiscal year. You hope that no one recognises you. The waiter asks to see your room key when you sign the bill, and he calls out the number to you in a voice loud enough for others to hear.

After dinner you are relieved to discover that your materials have been delivered to your room and placed on your bed. You do not have a knife to open the boxes. You call the porter again and ask for assistance. A young person comes and opens the boxes for you. You tip the porter and then begin arranging your materials on the bed according to the sessions in which you will use them. You have a checklist, and you discover that your nameplates and felt-tipped markers are missing. Also, page two of your Monday morning handout is duplicated, and there is no page three.

It is almost 10.00 p.m. so you decide to check on the training room. You become lost in a maze of corridors, find an empty seminar room with a telephone, call the front desk for more directions, and find your way to your assigned room. It is a disaster. There are windows on three sides, looking out over a marina, with sailing boats moored close by. The cleaning staff have taken away the dishes and tablecloths, but the large, round, bare tables are left, along with leftover programmes and rubbish on the floor. A 'head table' remains on a dais. There is no telephone. You find one and telephone the front desk again. By now they are treating you like a pest. You ask when your room will be set up, and they say that the catering staff arrives at 8.00 a.m. on Mondays. You decide to leave them implicit instructions on the room layout, so you draw a diagram and leave it on the head table. You will have to get to bed right away, since you know you will have to supervise the room set-up tomorrow morning.

Back in your bedroom you discover that you have forgotten to pack your shampoo. The kiosk that sells sundries in the hotel lobby has closed for the night. There is a loud party in the next room. You watch the news on television, hoping to distract yourself before falling asleep. After shutting off the set, you can tell that the party next door has disbanded, but the host has the television turned up loud. You telephone the front desk again, and they telephone your neighbour's room. You hear drunken swearing in reply. Somehow you drift into fitful sleep, dreaming of uncovered tables.

Your alarm call is fifteen minutes late. You telephone room service immediately to have breakfast sent up. They promise to deliver it in about twenty minutes. Forty-five minutes later you call room service again to find out when your breakfast will arrive, and soon there is a knock on your door. The waiter brings in your tray. There is no newspaper, although you requested one, and you have been sent regular coffee instead of the decaffeinated variety that you asked for. You sign the bill, and the person tells you that no gratuity is included. You scramble to find a tip. It is 8.20 a.m. when you arrive at the seminar room. The course is scheduled to begin at 9.00 a.m., with reception beginning at 8.30 a.m. There is no registration table outside the room. You look in, and what you see is dismaying. There are straight rows of tables (covered, thank God), and a table for you on a dais. There is one flipchart, the floppy kind, and red and black crayons on the front table. A meeting has already started in the room next door. You can clearly hear the soundtrack of a film. One of the participants for your seminar shows up to register precisely at 8.30 a.m. She says that she had a hard time finding the room. You ask her to wait while you race to the lobby. There is no mention of your company's seminar on the lobby notice board. You speak to the porter, who indicates that there are messages for you at registration. One tells you that two of your sixteen participants will not attend, another informs you that a Mr Yablonsky will arrive at midday, and three others are for participants. You glance at these, and they all contain the same message: 'Call your office right away'.

Back at the seminar room you find four people waiting to register. One is smoking a foul cigar. Another greets you with, 'Where's the coffee?' It is 9.00 a.m. No coffee. No breakfast rolls. No rapport . . .

This series of disasters seems fictitious, but it is actually realistic. We have experienced more difficult situations in management development, but most were in foreign countries. The purpose of this chapter is to consider various dimensions of logistical planning for conducting effective management development courses. Murphy's Law states 'If anything can go wrong, it will'. We cited earlier the principle of five p's: 'poor planning precedes puny performance'. It is our view that the trainer needs to imagine all of the things that can possibly go wrong and to plan to meet these contingencies. Some anecdotes from our management development training experience might illustrate the importance of anticipating problems.

Managers were being sent to a mountain retreat for a seminar. We arrived three hours before, only to find that the training room had not been opened for several days. There had been a large snowfall, and a previous event had been cancelled. When we entered the room we were confronted with a horrible stench. The room was cold, and it was below freezing outside. The room was a basement, with small, high windows. We asked that the heat be turned on fully, and we began to investigate the source of the foul odour. Finally we found a dead rat behind a hole in one of the walls. This wall had to be dismantled, and the room had to be fumigated overnight. The afternoon and evening sessions on the first day had to be conducted in the dining room. Fortunately, the kitchen staff were understanding, and there were no other guests at the retreat.

For a management seminar in a New York school system our client had booked a religious retreat house. We arrived the night before the event was scheduled to start and made a pot of coffee for a last-minute staff meeting. The next morning that coffee pot would not work. People began arriving and were annoyed at not having their morning 'fix' of caffeine. The seminar began forty-five minutes late, and it took all day to establish minimal rapport with the participants.

The air-conditioning failed in a conference room we were using. The hotel was fully booked. We negotiated the use of a 'bridal suite', and we moved all the furniture out into the hall. The hotel was unhappy, but the seminar worked.

We were bombarded with noise from a presentation in an adjoining room in a prestigious hotel in Atlanta. After notes requesting consideration were ignored, we organised our group to give a rousing cheer just as soon as a break occurred in the other group's activities. It worked.

For showing a film at one conference centre, we turned off the room lights. What we did not know was that they were a special kind that takes about five minutes to come back on. We lost the impact of reactions from the film.

At a beachfront resort our training room was on the ground level, on the way out to the beach. Just outside the door was a pinball machine that looked innocuous enough during the daytime. During our opening session, however, children congregated around the machine, and we were serenaded by cheers, whirrs and clicks. The management refused to move the machine. There was a bar across the hall. During a coffee break some of our participants drank alcohol instead of coffee.

We were just about to have a mid-morning coffee break in a hotel conference room in Los Angeles when housekeeping personnel began taking the refreshments away. They did not speak English.

At a particularly significant moment in a management exercise, in which a lot of emotion had been elicited, the back door opened, and a uniformed lady rolled in a tea trolley. People immediately abandoned the activity and raced for the goodies. It was impossible to bring them back into the design effectively.

During a structured experience in which manager-participants were working in small groups to solve a personnel problem, one group was struggling particularly hard. When we intervened, we discovered that their materials were incomplete. The exercise required members to discover that they have different information and to share it. What had happened was that two participants had been inadvertently given the same data sheets. One page, then, was missing. Members of the group became immediately suspicious, accusing the trainer of deliberately setting them up for failure.

Over a lunch break one management development seminar participant broke his wrist in a fall while trying to learn how to use a skateboard. He had to be rushed to a hospital and then sent home.

Other anecdotes could be recounted, but probably these are enough to make the point. In this chapter we shall cover training site selection, site management, training room set-up, refreshments and meals, registration, and group-maintenance norms. The advice comes from our experience in having to deal with a formidable array of 'hitches' that jeopardise the effectiveness of management development courses.

SELECTING TRAINING SITES

When management development courses are held 'off-site', someone must make arrangements for space and services elsewhere. The best training design can be rendered ineffective by the site arrangements. Boone and Reid (1978) and Stewart and Stewart (1978) discuss the importance of actually visiting prospective sites before making contractual arrangements. The following important considerations should, we believe, be taken into account in deciding where the seminar will take place.

It is usually desirable to conduct management development courses away from the office. People tend to be less easily distracted by the day-to-day occurrences that are taking place in their work situations while the seminar is taking place. The place should be easily accessible by road, reasonably quiet, and attractive. There should be adequate security at the site and enough privacy to permit open discussion of organisational information. There should be plenty of parking space.

The seminar room itself should be big enough (allow about 25–35 square feet per participant minimum), well lit and with plenty of wall space for posting material. The room should be easily found by participants not familiar with the site. It should be located away from attractions such as bars, shops, and recreational areas. Cloakroom facilities should be close by. The room should have more than one entrance, preferably, so that participants can enter and leave through a back door. There should be windows, since some people tend towards claustrophobia in rooms without windows. Decorations in the room should not be distracting. Ideally the room should be carpeted, and have sound-absorbent curtains. There should be a temperature control device in the room and no telephone. Avoid long, narrow rooms that have a 'bowling alley' feel to them.

'Breakout' rooms located near the main seminar room are desirable in some course designs. (In some countries these are referred to as 'syndicate' rooms, a term that has pejorative connotations in the United States.) These rooms should be equipped with flipcharts and/or blackboards, tables and chairs. All rooms should have adequate electrical outlets.

Contracting with a training site can be hazardous, in that the two parties are in very different businesses. This is a part of site selection because during this activity you have to develop a subjective 'feel' for how personnel at the site are likely to respond to your requests and demands. Their management philosophy has to be somewhat compatible with what you are exposing managers to in your seminar. Ask for perks, such as a bedroom for yourself, use of equipment, supplies such as newsprint and markers, services such as photocopying. Check the accessibility of key staff or site. Find out who are the back-up staff in out-of-work hours.

SITE MANAGEMENT

On-site management of the seminar arrangements is necessary to ensure that the contract is carried out and adjusted appropriately. It is often helpful to imagine that the site is disorganised (which, unfortunately, seems often to be the case) and that you will have to provide linkages among its components. In a hotel, for example, there are 'empires': registration, porters, the dining room, the coffee shop, housekeeping, maintenance (sometimes called engineering), sales (sometimes named catering), etc. Often personnel do not communicate well across their territorial boundaries. Sometimes there are jurisdictional disputes, exacerbated by the presence of several unions, and occasionally these areas are staffed by different companies. Do not expect hotels to co-ordinate any arrangements. Double and triple check every arrangement. The following considerations need to be taken into account to make sure that the site supports the seminar.

A primary contact person is mandatory. Have one individual who will see to it that the arrangements in your contract are provided adequately and promptly. Nurture this person. Have one or more back-up contacts identified for times when the primary person is not available. Get yourself introduced to these persons. Often the staff changes completely on weekends. Find out how you can make emergency contact with your primary contact person at home, if necessary, if the seminar or your stay encompasses any time on Saturday and Sunday. When there is more than one staff member, we strongly prefer to divide responsibilities. One person handles all contacts with the site – before, during, and after the seminar. Another trainer has primary accountability for the quality of the learning event; he or she runs all staff meetings, for example.

Find out what the house rules and standard operating procedures are. Sometimes there are quiet hours, no-posting policies, no-alcohol laws, and labour contracts that can prohibit you from setting up your own equipment or even opening crates. Find out whether all participants' room charges can be centralised and billed to your company. Make sure that participants will have to pay their own bar bills, if that is your company's policy. Find out about any regulations relating to parking and to room checkout. If your seminar closes after room checkout time, you may negotiate a late checkout for the entire group. Be certain that you understand how the message system works, and make a strong request that your sessions are not interrupted. Ask how participants' complaints about their rooms and service are to be handled.

See about the availability of secretarial and photocopying services at the site. Make a request that such charges be added to your central account. Find out how you can get emergency assistance for your audiovisual equipment. Bring along extra bulbs for projectors. If the seminar room is not cleaned, or it is rearranged incorrectly by the house staff, have a direct contact set up for a fast remedy.

TRAINING ROOM PREPARATION

There is no substitute for meticulous care in setting up training rooms for management development seminars. That is why it is vital always to arrive hours before the event is due to begin. Firstly, the room needs to be made spotless. Artwork may have to be removed. Surplus furniture will need to be taken out. The floor will need cleaning thoroughly. Flipcharts will require fresh pads of newsprint. Blackboards will need to be washed and each seat and table inspected. The temperature control device should be tested. The functioning of curtain and window openers should be checked. The furniture will have to be arranged, and nameplates and writing supplies made available for participants. The training materials will be arranged on a side table in the order in which they are going to be used. Audiovisual equipment will be installed and tested. Extension electrical cords should be taped to the floor so that people will not trip over them. Working posters will be made on a flipchart. Doors will be checked to make sure that exits are clear. Cloakrooms must be checked for cleanliness. Last minute preparations for refreshments should be double-checked.

Our system is to use learning teams in management development

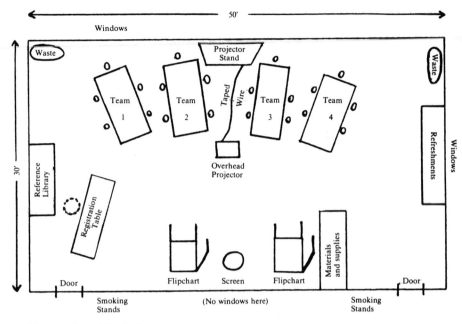

Figure 6.1   Training room set-up

courses, and we arrange the seminar room accordingly. We want the members of a team to sit together around a work table, and we want the teams close enough to each other so that all participants can easily see our audiovisual presentation and hear each other in total group discussions. Our most common seminar room set-up, then, looks like the layout in Figure 6.1.

Several features of this plan need to be pointed out. Participants should be seated looking away from windows. There should usually be no physical barrier between the trainer and the participants, since this tends to reinforce teacher-student role-taking and produce psychological distance. Refreshments should be available continually, away from work tables; they should be situated so that the site staff can replenish them without undue disruption. A table for reference materials for participants to browse through is placed opposite the refreshments, to avoid accidental spillage on books and other displayed matter. The film/videotape relay/slide stand is placed at the rear of the room so that it does not visually distract from the screen. (The overhead projector is stored on the side of the room except when it is rolled into the centre for actual use.) Training materials are placed at the side of the trainer, so that notes can be easily consulted and handouts are at the ready. Also, extra felt-tipped markers, masking tape, blu-tack, and other supplies should be close at hand. Lights just over the screen are turned off when the screen is in use. Make sure that there is plenty of light on you and your charts. Curtains and blinds are nearly closed. A sign on one of the flipcharts says, 'Welcome to the Management Development Seminar. Thank you for not smoking'. We like to play music while people are assembling and during breaks, so a cassette tape player is placed on the trainer's materials table. All ashtrays are taken out of the room and placed in the hall outside. Since all of this work on setting up the seminar room requires the utmost co-operation of the site staff, we tend to tip them generously before they begin. They expect, and receive, another generous gratuity when the seminar is over.

Breakout rooms are arranged to facilitate egalitarian exchange. There is simply a table around which are arranged a sufficient number of chairs. We prefer to have writing materials, felt-tipped pens (several colours), and a flipchart in each room.

REFRESHMENTS AND MEALS

We have indicated that we strongly prefer that refreshments be present when participants arrive and that they remain available continuously. This helps managers to feel comfortable at the beginning of sessions, and it gives us flexibility in scheduling breaks during the programme. Also, we tend to establish an informal atmosphere, encouraging people to take refreshments whenever they wish.

The traditional refreshments in the United States are coffee, hot tea, and 'sweet rolls' in the morning, sometimes accompanied by thick cream, caffeinc-free coffee, and orange juice. In the UK, coffee and biscuits are usually served. We prefer to have a bowl of fresh fruit, coffee, decaffeinated coffee, sugar, cream, saccharine, non-dairy creamer, juice and herb teas present. This gives people who are addicted to sugar and caffeine what they need, and it provides sensible alternatives. Our experience is that people often begin to choose the healthier options during the seminar. We do not comment.

It is important to consider a policy on alcohol. This substance does not mix well with training. Our policy is for there to be no drinking of alcohol until the training day is completed. We serve alcohol only at formal meals and perhaps after an evening training session. We also urge participants not to take alcohol during the day. We may join the group at the bar for a nightcap, but we want the management development course itself not to be associated with drinking. Another policy that we hold is that drinkers pay for their own alcohol. This keeps the costs of the training down and avoids criticisms. Of course, participants need to know this policy in advance of their attendance.

Group meals can be time-consuming and expensive. Usually the site makes a significant amount of its profit on these services and they attempt to sell you more than you need. If you opt for group meals, have the room not adjacent to the seminar room; the noise of setting-up meals can be a serious distraction. Let participants be on their own for breakfast and dinner, which can drag on for hours, and schedule a light lunch to consist of soup and salad, or light sandwiches, with no alcohol. Caution managers not to discuss confidential organisational matters in public areas. In scheduling meals take into account the special dietary requirements of participants. Some may be vegetarians, some may be on special diets, others may have religious restrictions, etc. This should be handled discreetly, by alerting the site staff in private as to who receives what food.

If the seminar is designed to be residential and will last a week, you may want to have a formal meal on the last evening before the final session. This event can be preceded by cocktails, and the programme could include an address by a prominent company executive. Team awards can be presented, with each team honouring each other member of another team and the training staff. It is important that this event points towards the closing session so that participants do not 'shut down' too early.

RECREATION

Management development courses usually involve sitting for long periods. There should be provisions for physical 'changes of pace'. We prefer to have a recreation break planned into the schedule each day, with a competitive activity, such as volleyball, in which almost all participate. Volleyball is almost ideal, since it can be fun even if participants have never played. Up to twelve persons can be on a side, and the exercise is not strenuous. We also facilitate people with similar interests, such as jogging or tennis, to meet each other to plan joint recreation activities in their own time. If there are no recreational facilities available on-site, we plan to include brief 'energisers' into the training design.

Evening recreational activities can include cards, table tennis, voluntary informal discussions, optional sessions, motivational movies, darts, and the like. These evening get-togethers can have a strong integrative effect on the group.

REGISTRATION

It is critical that each participant be greeted cordially and 'signed in' with a minimum of fuss. We prefer for course participants to be pre-registered, so that we can make up a roster to be distributed to them on arrival. Then they only have to check in at the seminar room before the event begins.

Before a management development course starts, the training staff is usually pre-occupied with all of the arrangements and the programme. Consequently, they may appear to be cold or uninterested in the participants. Under these conditions we believe that it is good practice to have someone else serve as receptionist for the course. This can be a clerical employee of the company, perhaps the secretary of the training department, or a site staff member. Each participant is greeted warmly and given last-minute instructions in a warm manner. The trainer(s) then greet each participant also.

The registration table should be placed just inside the seminar room until it is time for the course to begin. Then it is moved outside into the hall for latecomers. It is our firm belief that all sessions should begin on time, regardless of how many people are present. This establishes a norm of punctuality and puts the 'reward system' in perspective. Beginning late rewards coming late and punishes punctuality.

At registration participants are given a name tag prepared by the registrar, with large block lettered first names. They also receive a roster of participants and an agenda, or schedule. They may also be given a task to perform before the training starts, such as reading, filling-in a questionnaire, etc. They are directed to the refreshments table. They may be introduced to other participants who are nearby. Use their names a lot in the beginning, in order to begin learning them.

GROUP MAINTENANCE NORMS

In planning management development courses it is important to consider how to establish norms, or expectations, on the part of participants. The pre-registration, or orientation, is critical. The memoranda that are distributed prior to the course should reduce the 'expectation gap' that can exist in the opening session of the course. People need to know that there will be no smoking in the sessions but that there will be frequent breaks, that no alcohol will be consumed until after hours, that telephone messages will not interrupt the sessions except for dire emergencies, that there will be planned recreation, that the sessions will stress hard, practical problem solving, and so on. We encourage managers not to arrive very early. These norms need to be re-stressed during the opening session.

Our practice of establishing committees to take care of refreshments, the appearance of the room, etc., in the opening session helps to establish the norm that as adults we take responsibility for the total learning environment. We plan to have frequent breaks of about fifteen minutes each, and we discourage participants from making telephone calls during the breaks.

When the room needs to be rearranged for a particular activity, we use participants. They almost always respond positively to the statement, 'I need your help'.

One technique that we often use to infuse humour, energy, and competition into the team arrangement is 'Noogies'. We have frequent 'trivia contests', at the beginning of sessions or after breaks, and award 'Noogies' to all teams that have correct responses within the time allowed (usually only a few seconds). Then we take away a 'Noogie' when the entire team is not seated at its table at appointed times. The winning team receives special recognition at the final meal or in the closing session. The effect of this technique is to cause teams to 'shape up' each other's behaviour.

Sometimes acts of God intervene. Power failures, fires, storms, etc., can seriously disrupt the proceedings. Remember that whatever happens, the group did not do it to you. You must share the responsibility for coping with any unforeseen events.

When the training is to be offered in-house, that is, on the organisation's property, it is often helpful to establish a 'thousand mile rule': imagine that you are one thousand miles away from the office, in a wooded retreat, with no telephones. One organisation in which we worked established such a rule for a special seminar room constructed above the manufacturing floor. The room was self-contained, with its own cloakroom, kitchen, air conditioner, etc. All employees were notified not to disturb what happened in the room unless there was a true emergency.

LOGISTICAL PLANNING WORKSHEETS

The two instruments that follow are intended to be used before the event actually begins. The first is a checklist of considerations and information on the site itself, and it may be helpful in selecting sites and in keeping a file of sites. The second focuses on the arrangements for the event itself, and it may be helpful in avoiding administrative mistakes and in filing for the requirements of the course, in case someone else will conduct the training later.

We recommend that the trainer fill out the first inventory, the training site worksheet, during a site visit. The second inventory is begun as soon as the site is selected and becomes a guide for all administrative and logistical arrangements. We believe that the trainer(s) should consult the second form frequently just before the event begins. Another good practice is to have a copy of the actual contract with the site on hand at all times during the course. The goal is: No surprises.

This chapter has been highly opinionated, and we do not apologise for that. Obviously, we vary our professional practice according to particular courses, participants, sites, schedules, etc. What we have presented works most often in our experience.

REFERENCES

Boone, T. A. and Reid, R. A. 'Selecting Workshop Sites' in Pfeiffer, J. W. and Jones, J. E. (eds) *The 1978 Annual Handbook for Group Facilitators*, San Diego, CA: University Associates, 1978.

Stewart, V. and Stewart, A. 'Good Housekeeping for Internal Courses' Chapter 9 in *Managing the Manager's Growth*, Aldershot, England: Gower, 1978.

TRAINING SITE WORKSHEET

Instructions

Fill out this form during a site visit. Use it as the basis for contracting with the site. File the worksheet for future reference and for use during management development courses.

Date ....

Name ....

1   Name of training site ....

2   Address ....
    ....
    ....

3   Main contact person ....
    Title ....
    Telephone ....

4   Back-up person ....
    Title ....
    Telephone ....

5   Person in charge of seminar room set-up ....
    Title ....
    Telephone ....

6   Person in charge of refreshments/meals ....
    Title ....
    Telephone ....

7   General concerns checklist
    Accessibility ....
    Attractiveness to participants ....
    Availability of photocopying services ....
    Availability of secretarial services ....
    Deposit needed for reservation ....
    Emergency assistance ....
    Fire prevention ....
    Guarantees ....
    Handling participants' complaints ....
    House rules ....
    Internal noise level ....

Recreation facilities and equipment . . . .
Security . . . .
Temperature . . . .
Lobby marquee and directions to seminar rooms . . . .
Medical support . . . .
Message system . . . .
Night staffing . . . .
On-site supplies, such as newsprint . . . .
Other events scheduled at the same time . . . .
Outside noise level . . . .
Parking . . . .
Philosophy of site staff . . . .
Prices . . . .
Privacy . . . .
Transportation to site . . . .
Weekend staffing . . . .

8   Seminar rooms checklist

Acessibility from other site areas such as dining or bedrooms,
    parking . . . .
Attractiveness . . . .
Audiovisual equipment . . . .
Audiovisual screens . . . .
Breakfast rooms . . . .
Decorations . . . .
Curtains, blinds . . . .
Electrical outlets . . . .
Entrances . . . .
Flipcharts . . . .
Lighting . . . .
Lighting controls . . . .
Location *vis-à-vis* nuisances such as bars, shops . . . .
Proximity to cloakrooms . . . .
Security . . . .
Shape . . . .
Size . . . .
Sound insulation . . . .
Telephone . . . .
Temperature control device . . . .
Wall space . . . .
Windows . . . .

9   Refreshments and meals checklist

Appropriate menu in dining room ....
Availability of alternatives, such as fruit, juice, non-caffeine
    drinks, tea, etc. ....
Flexibility in handling variable numbers of participants

....
Food quality ....
Keeping refreshments supplied ....
Provision for special diets ....
Quick service ....
Separate dining room ....

10   Bedrooms checklist

Advance registration ....
Bar bills and other room charges such as room service, tele-
    phone, laundry, TV-films, etc. ....
Co-ordinated billing ....
Participants' bedrooms
Room checkout time *vis-à-vis* seminar's scheduled closing ....
Trainer's bedroom

11   Overall impressions

LOGISTICAL PLANNING WORKSHEET

Instructions

Use this worksheet before and during the management development course to make sure that you have 'covered all the bases'. Use it in conjunction with the training site worksheet for the actual site chosen for the event.

Course

_____

Dates

1   Materials and supplies checklist

_____ Duct tape for affixing electrical cords to the floor
_____ Emergency medical supplies
_____ Expendable training materials, laid out in order
_____ Felt-tipped markers
_____ Handouts, laid out in order
_____ Hole punch
_____ Masking tape
_____ Name tapes
_____ Newsprint
_____ Printed agenda

_____ Prizes and/or awards
_____ Recreational materials
_____ Registration materials
_____ Resource library
_____ Roster
_____ Signs
_____ Special pens for overhead transparencies
_____ Stapler
_____ Writing supplies

2   Registrar

_____ Orientation
_____ Materials

_____ Location
_____ Contingencies

3   Seminar room arrangements checklist

_____ Furniture arranged and checked
_____ Doors unlocked
_____ Temperature adjusted
_____ Audiovisual equipment installed

_____ Lighting checked
_____ Curtains/blinds checked
_____ Floor, walls, furniture cleaned
_____ Flipcharts equipped with new pads of newsprint

____ Electrical cords secured   ____ Breakout rooms prepared
____ Nameplates distributed   ____ Film/slides cued up
____ Writing materials   ____ Fire exits noted
          distributed

4   Front desk checklist

____ Roster of participants   ____ Assumptions about
          supplied   billings checked
____ Personnel oriented to   ____ Message system checked
          give instructions
____ Lobby marquee checked

5   Cloakroom checklist

____ Sanitary   ____ Graffiti erased
____ Proper paper and soap
          supplied

6   Refreshments checklist

____ Contracted schedule   ____ Milk
          checked   ____ Sugar
____ Prices checked   ____ Saccharine
____ Coffee   ____ Honey
____ Decaffeinated coffee   ____ Fruit
____ Tea, both with and without   ____ Juice
          caffeine   ____ Rolls
____ Cups

7   Meals room checklist

____ Location   ____ Menu checked
____ Schedule checked   ____ Final dinner planned

7 Evaluating management development sessions

Since we focused in Chapter 1 on evaluating management development *programmes,* in this chapter we shall be concerned solely with the evaluation of *sessions* – courses, seminars, workshops, and other such presentations. We shall discuss the motives for carrying out session evaluations and some common methods for studying the outcomes of trainings. This chapter will include several instruments: a form for evaluating individual presentations in sessions in which there is a series of staff inputs, an end-of-course assessment form, a scale for studying changes in the managerial effectiveness of participants as viewed by themselves and by others, and a sample pair of follow-up survey questionnaires to be filled out by participants and their supervisors.

MOTIVES FOR EVALUATION

There are three primary reasons for conducting evaluation studies of management development sessions: political, programmatic, and pay-off. Each motive is legitimate, and probably all three should stimulate the gathering and analysis of data within organisations.

Political

Political motives include the desire for the programme to survive within the organisation, the interest in keeping one's management development position, and the need to develop senior management support for the programme. Data are assembled to provide for protection, continuance and endorsement of the effort. This is the 'show and tell' dimension of session evaluations: here's what people said about the programme, here's what it's doing for us, etc. Management development personnel need to be sensitive to the need to provide 'objective' data to senior management about the sessions so as to justify ongoing operations.

Programmatic

Programmatic motives include the need for data to evaluate desirable design changes in sessions and the interest in providing feedback to presenters on how well they worked in the learning activities. Every seminar, course, workshop, etc., should include experimental elements (trying it another way), and these need to be evaluated. Programmatic evaluations are usually conducted by and for the management development staff.

Pay-off

Pay-off motives include the need to study the transfer of training to on-the-job behaviour, the interest in assessing long-term effects of management development sessions, and the desire to determine the overall effect on the organisation of the cumulative array of training activities. Of course, the ultimate justification for conducting learning activities is their actual impact on the effectiveness of the system. Often it is assumed that if the individual manager benefits, the organisation *ipso facto* does. These motives dictate the evaluative methods to be employed in session assessment. The next section outlines the most common approaches that are in use in evaluating management development sessions.

COMMON EVALUATIVE METHODS

The most often used evaluative strategies include end-of-course ratings/testimonials, following surveys, following interviews, following meetings, and monitoring 'hard' indexes. Each of these strategies will be discussed in turn. Undoubtedly any thorough study of the effectiveness of management development sessions would incorporate more than one of these common methods.

End-of-course evaluations

These give the staff quick feedback on the short-term effects of the learning activities, but this method is notorious for generating inflatedly positive statistics. People who stay to the end of a session are likely to rate it highly. Hence, the data are often useful when the motive for evaluation is primarily political. A variation on this method is the end-of-presentation evaluation, used when a session consists of a sequence of staff presentations on different topics. Participants are asked to evaluate a given speaker, or presenter. The advantage of this approach is to obtain data while the memory of the presentation is still fresh. The main disadvantages include a loss of overall perspective and a tendency to confuse content and style in rating presenters.

Following surveys

These entail distributing questionnaires to management development session participants after they have been back on the job for a month or so after the training. This method is an effective way of determining some of the lasting effects of the training. Sometimes instruments are also distributed to other people who interact with participants – their supervisors, colleagues, and subordinates. One disadvantage of this method is that it is sometimes difficult to obtain a high percentage of response. An example of a thorough application of this method is the Management Development Audit, developed in England by Easterby-Smith, Braiden and Ashton (1980).

Following interviews

These are sometimes carried out with management development session attendees. These can be conducted with individuals and/or small groups, but the most common approach is one-to-one. Such interviews can unearth subtle effects of the training and can permit managers to evaluate the training in their own words. An additional advantage of this strategy is that it can easily provide the opportunity for coaching and counselling. Concepts and skills learned in management development sessions are not always readily transferable to real-world situations, and sometimes managers need consultative assistance in applying what they have learned.

Following meetings

These are sometimes held to reinforce learnings developed in courses and seminars. These meetings can have a strong supportive effect on participants. People help each other apply their new knowledge and skill in practical situations. These meetings can, however, develop the flavour of a 'class reunion', and it is important to conduct them in a way that balances needs for celebration and for further learning.

Monitoring 'hard' indexes

This means studying the operating statistics of the organisation to determine the effects of management development sessions. Such data might include information on staff turnover, absenteeism, use of health facilities, cost reductions, productivity, profitability, promotions, etc. These are generally considered non-reactive measures; that is, the programme participant is not being asked to respond directly. Of course, these statistics are affected by almost everything that occurs within the organisation, so they have to be interpreted carefully regarding the unique effects of management development activities.

As in the case of training needs assessments, discussed in Chapter 3, mixed methods are probably best in evaluating the outcomes of management development sessions. Some mix of interviews, questionnaires, meetings, and study of ongoing-operation measures needs to be devised in keeping with the purposes of the evaluation. Of course, all of this is facilitated by planning the evaluation *before* conducting the sessions, when considerations of purpose are likely to be considered carefully.

FIVE USEFUL INSTRUMENTS

In this section we present sample instruments that can in most cases be used either as they are or be modified easily to fit the purposes of evaluating particular management development sessions. Three have been devised for this volume, and two come from a large-scale study conducted by John E. Jones in an organisation in the United States. A combination of these instruments can be employed in comprehensive studies of the effects of training.

Management development presenter evaluation form

This instrument is designed to be used after each major speaker or presenter in sessions that feature a succession of inputs by different staff. The form facilitates comparisons between presenters and across time, to measure improvement in delivering content. The ratings are standardised on ten-point scales. The distinction between content and style may have to be explained orally, along with the purposes for using the instrument. We recommend that statistical summaries be made, shared with presenters, and filed. Obviously, the information generated by this method is inadequate to determine the overall effects of the session, so it is strongly recommended that this form is not used as the sole means of evaluation. In using the instrument, as with all of the others, it is important to have participants respond individually, before talking with each other about the presentation. This cuts down on data contamination.

Management development session feedback form

This instrument is designed to be used at the end of a training course. It permits comparisons between courses and across time for a given course, to measure improvement in programme delivery. The same ten-point-scale feature is incorporated, along with free response format items in order to capture the short-term evaluative feelings of participants. The ratings are likely to be inflated and need to be interpreted cautiously. Responses to item 3 can be useful in planning course changes, and data generated by the final item can be used in advertising the next offering of the session. Participants are asked to put their names on this form, in contrast to the presenter-evaluation one. We have found it useful to ask respondents not to make tasteless remarks about the training – no criticisms that may be unfair or improper. A good rule of practice in conducting management development sessions is to state early that an end-of-course evaluation will be conducted and that it is hoped that there are no surprises in the data. Participants are encouraged to share their criticisms at appropriate times throughout the session.

Management development participant analysis form

This instrument is designed to study the pre-post changes that managers experience in training. It can be filled out by the participants themselves, their supervisors, colleagues/peers, subordinates, spouses, etc. Several possible applications are possible. One or two weeks before the session participants can be asked to complete the scale and to distribute copies to 'significant others' who are qualified to describe him/her. Each instrument is accompanied by a return envelope addressed to the session co-ordinator. The data are collated for each participant and fed back confidentially early in the programme, in order to facilitate personal/ professional goal setting. Then the process is repeated about two months after the session in order to chart changes. A variation is to omit the in-session feedback and to have private interviews with participants after the second assessment. This instrument requires a significant amount of data manipulation, so it may be desirable to ask the data processing department to write a special computer program to generate individual profiles.

Management seminar follow-up survey

This is a pair of instruments that was designed for a postal survey to study the training conducted by a large computer services company in the United States. One form is for participants, and the parallel one is for their supervisors. Sample computer-generated bar charts are included. These instruments are included in this chapter as examples of how to take the curriculum and objectives of a given management development session and convert it to a standardised questionnaire. Notice that some items are common to the two forms of the instrument, permitting comparisons of evaluations by participants and their supervisors. In the study, incidentally, almost every feature of the seminar was rated more highly by attendees than by their supervisors. Of course, this technique can be adapted to include data solicited from subordinates also. The instrument features a unique variation on the five-point Likert scale, stretching it to ten points.

A FINAL NOTE

Evaluating the outcomes of management development is hard work. It involves developing schemes to generate reliable, valid numbers, collecting masses of information, sifting through to discover trends, conducting experiments, providing feedback, and so on. The effort is essential, however, and it should be undertaken *continuously.*

This book has presented our judgements about how management development is best conducted. Our exposition has included the strongly held belief that packaged training is almost always inappropriate for the organisation. All of the materials and models need to be adapted to the needs of a particular system. Almost all senior managers subscribe to the philosophy that 'people are our most important asset'. We believe that the development of competence among managers is one of the very best ways of developing organisational resources.

REFERENCE

Easterby-Smith, M., Braiden, E. and Ashton, D. *Auditing Management Development,* Aldershot, England: Gower, 1980.

MANAGEMENT DEVELOPMENT PRESENTER
EVALUATION FORM

Name of Presenter _____

Today's date _____

For Programme and Staff Improvement

Instructions

Please provide the following feedback to the presenter, who will be given a summary of the results. The purpose of this assessment is to ensure that each presenter receives accurate data concerning his/her part in the management development session. You are asked to comment on the *content* of the presentation and the presenter's *style,* or manner of presentation.

CONTENT (Circle ratings and add comments.)

A   *Relevance* to your work:

1   2   3   4   5   6   7   8   9   10
Not very   Highly
relevant to   relevant to
my work   my work

Comment: _____

_____

B   *Organisation* of the material:

1   2   3   4   5   6   7   8   9   10
Not well   Very well
organised   organised
for me   for me

Comment: _____

_____

C   *Delivery* of the material:

| 1 | 2 | 3 | 4 | 5 | 6 | 7 | 8 | 9 | 10 |

Inadequately   Adequately
designed   designed
delivery   delivery

Comment: _____

_____

D   How might the presenter improve this material? _____

_____

STYLE (Circle ratings and add comments.)

E   *Rapport* with participants:

| 1 | 2 | 3 | 4 | 5 | 6 | 7 | 8 | 9 | 10 |

Not very much   Very good
in contact with   relationship
participants   with us

Comment: _____

_____

F   *Manner* of presentation:

| 1 | 2 | 3 | 4 | 5 | 6 | 7 | 8 | 9 | 10 |

Dull and   Interesting
boring   and stimulating

Comment: _____

_____

G   How might the presenter improve in his/her style? _____

_____

Thank you for your co-operation in providing this feedback to the
presenter and to the management development staff.

MANAGEMENT DEVELOPMENT SESSION
FEEDBACK FORM

For Programme and Staff Improvement

Title of Session _____

Your Name _____

Today's date _____

1 Rate how *useful* this session was in helping you to learn things
   that you can use in your work right now. Circle a number on the
   scale and add any comment you wish under it.

1   2   3   4   5   6   7   8   9   10

This session did not   This session helped me
help me to learn many   to learn many useful
useful things for my work   things for my work

Comment:

2 Rate your *satisfaction* with how the staff conducted the session.

1   2   3   4   5   6   7   8   9   10

Not very satisfied   Very satisfied

Comment:

3 What would have had to happen in order for your ratings to be
   10s?

Usefulness

Staff Conduct

4   What was the impact of this session on you as a participant?

Thank you for your co-operation in providing this feedback to the management development staff.

Confidential

MANAGEMENT DEVELOPMENT PARTICIPANT ANALYSIS FORM

For programme and participant improvement

Name of programme participant

_____

Today's date _____

Your relationship to this person (mark one only):

1 ☐ These are self ratings.
2 ☐ This person supervises me.
3 ☐ I am a colleague/peer of this person.
4 ☐ I supervise this person.

Instructions

The person named on this form is involved in a management development programme. This form will permit a study of how he/she is perceived by others in the work situation right now. The information will be useful both to the individual named and to the management development staff in evaluating the effects of learning activities. Please give your candid assessment of this person as you are experiencing him/her at this time. The anonymous data will be collated and presented to the participant in a confidential report. Do not put your name on this form. Return it to the Director, Management development. Indicate your perception of the participant by circling the number corresponding to each of the following items. Leave blank any items for which you do not feel qualified to respond or which seem not to be relevant to this person's work.

	Strongly disagree / Definitely not like him/her	Disagree / Unlike this person	Slightly disagree / Somewhat unlike him/her	Neither disagree nor agree	Slightly agree / Somewhat like him/her	Agree / Like this person	Strongly agree / Definitely like him/her
A Involves others appropriately in decisions that affect them	0	1	2	3	4	5	6
B Conducts effective meetings	0	1	2	3	4	5	6
C Is goal-directed	0	1	2	3	4	5	6

		Strongly disagree / Definitely not like him/her	Disagree / Unlike this person	Slightly disagree / Somewhat unlike him/her	Neither disagree nor agree	Slightly agree / Somewhat like him/her	Agree / Like this person	Strongly agree / Definitely like him/her
D	Provides appropriate feedback to others on the effects of their behaviour	0	1	2	3	4	5	6
E	Co-operates with others on problem solving	0	1	2	3	4	5	6
F	Delegates tasks effectively	0	1	2	3	4	5	6
G	Gives recognition to others for their accomplishments	0	1	2	3	4	5	6
H	Develops effective teamwork	0	1	2	3	4	5	6
I	Expresses feelings appropriately	0	1	2	3	4	5	6
J	Finds innovative ways to overcome barriers to goal attainment	0	1	2	3	4	5	6
K	Solicits reactions to his/her behaviour	0	1	2	3	4	5	6
L	Develops subordinate abilities effectively	0	1	2	3	4	5	6
M	Provides perspective for job tasks	0	1	2	3	4	5	6
N	Manages others in a flexible manner	0	1	2	3	4	5	6
O	Consults effectively with individuals on problems	0	1	2	3	4	5	6
P	Inspires subordinates to be productive	0	1	2	3	4	5	6
Q	Gives job task instructions effectively	0	1	2	3	4	5	6

		Strongly disagree / Definitely not like him/her	Disagree / Unlike this person	Slightly disagree / Somewhat unlike him/her	Neither disagree nor agree	Slightly agree / Somewhat like him/her	Agree / Like this person	Strongly agree / Definitely like him/her
R	Clarifies organisational values	0	1	2	3	4	5	6
S	Makes his/her expectations of others clear	0	1	2	3	4	5	6
T	Rewards superior effort appropriately	0	1	2	3	4	5	6
U	Mediates disputes effectively	0	1	2	3	4	5	6
V	Manages time effectively	0	1	2	3	4	5	6
W	Maintains employee discipline	0	1	2	3	4	5	6
X	Plans effectively	0	1	2	3	4	5	6
Y	Relates effectively to people outside the organisation	0	1	2	3	4	5	6
Z	Manages his/her personal and professional development effectively	0	1	2	3	4	5	6

Thank you for your co-operation in this confidential study.
Return this form in the envelope provided.

Personal and confidential
Urgent: Return by _____

MANAGEMENT SEMINAR FOLLOW-UP SURVEY

Code: _____

Participants' form

XYZ is engaged in a comprehensive study of all of its management development efforts. You attended the management seminar during the past few months, and we are interested in determining how useful the seminar was for you as a manager. It is important that you be candid in this assessment, since your data will be used to improve seminars that we shall be conducting during the coming months.

This questionnaire is coded, but your responses will be pooled with others' to study patterns and trends. You will not be individually identifiable in the analysis of the data.

For each of the following items simply mark what is true *for you*. Use this ten-point scale for your responses:

10	To a very great extent
8	To a great extent
6	To some extent
4	To a little extent
2	To a very little extent

You may use in-between (odd) numbers as well, but do not use zero. Write the number at the end of each of the following items. Then return this form in the enclosed envelope.

To what extent did the management seminar instruct you adequately in the following areas?

1 Affirmative action programme and equal employment opportunity ☐
2 Safety ☐
3 New products/engineering/equipment ☐
4 Employee benefits ☐
5 Appraisal interview ☐

6   Budgeting and accounting   ☐
7   Estimating   ☐
8   Order entry   ☐
9   Conference leadership   ☐
10 Operations   ☐
11 Interviewing, testing and hiring   ☐
12 Labour relations   ☐
13 Reading and interpreting manufacturing reports   ☐
14 Quality control procedures   ☐
15 Sales organisation   ☐
16 To what extent did the management seminar increase your
    confidence as a manager?   ☐
17 To what degree did the seminar improve your effectiveness
    as a manager?   ☐
18 To what degree did attendance at this seminar boost your
    morale?   ☐
19 To what extent did going to this seminar make you feel
    better about working for XYZ?   ☐
20 To what extent did this seminar make you feel more proud
    of the XYZ product?   ☐
21 To what degree did the seminar increase your sense of
    loyalty to XYZ?   ☐
22 To what extent were you impressed by the calibre of others
    who attended the seminar with you?   ☐

To determine the relevance of the content of the seminar for XYZ
managers like yourself, indicate below the extent to which you are
involved in each of the following activities:

23 Affirmative Action Programme and Equal Employment
    Opportunity   ☐
24 Safety   ☐
25 Engineering   ☐
26 Employee benefits   ☐
27 Appraisal interviews   ☐
28 Budgeting and accounting   ☐
29 Estimating   ☐
30 Order entry   ☐
31 Conference leadership   ☐
32 Operations   ☐
33 Reading and interpreting manufacturing reports   ☐
34 Quality control procedures   ☐

35 Sales   ☐
36 Interviewing, testing and hiring   ☐
37 Labour relations   ☐

Below are listed all of the instructors who were involved in the seminar you attended. Using the same 10-point scale, indicate the degree to which each *that you remember clearly* was effective as a presenter in the seminar. (Leave blank those presenters whom you do not remember clearly.)

38 Bill Anderson (Estimating and order entry)   ☐
39 Joe Billings (Budgeting and accounting)   ☐
40 Tom Bremingham (Co-ordination of course, conference
    leadership, etc.)   ☐
41 Mr. Cash (Senior executive question and answer session) ☐
42 Sally Demington (Budgeting and accounting)   ☐
43 David Hall (Budgeting and accounting)
44 Jack Hoving (Course summary, issuance of certificates)   ☐
45 Allan Hughes (Estimating and order entry)   ☐
46 Don Ivery (New products/equipment/engineering)   ☐
47 Joe Kenston (New products/equipment/engineering)   ☐
48 Mike Leary (Budgeting and accounting)   ☐
49 Ed Moore (Quality control procedures)   ☐
50 Nancy O'Shaughnessy (Reading and interpreting manu-
    facturing reports)   ☐
51 Lou Pullman (AAP/EEO, Safety)   ☐
·52 Tom Rodin (Interviewing, testing and hiring)   ☐
53 Joe Smith (Sales organisation)   ☐

Suggestions for improving the management seminar:

Return this questionnaire to:
Director,
Management Development,
XYZ Corporate Headquarters.

Thank you for your co-operation in this important study.

XYZ ORGANISATION MANAGEMENT SEMINAR SURVEY

Participant = 55

Affirmative action, equal employment opportunity

Item 1   Respondents = 53   Mean = 8.1   Std. Dev. = 1.22

Value	Freq.	%	0...1...2...3...4...5...6...7...8...9...0
10	10	18.9	*******
9	3	5.7	***
8	29	54.7	**********************
7	3	5.7	***
6	8	15.1	*******
5	0	0.0	
4	0	0.0	
3	0	0.0	
2	0	0.0	
1	0	0.0	

Safety

Item 2   Respondents = 53   Mean = 7.2   Std. Dev. = 1.74

Value	Freq.	%	0...1...2...3...4...5...6...7...8...9...0
10	7	13.2	******
9	1	1.9	*
8	18	34.0	*************
7	6	11.3	******
6	17	32.1	*************
5	1	1.9	*
4	2	3.8	**
3	0	0.0	
2	0	0.0	
1	1	1.9	*

New products/engineering/equipment

Item 3   Respondents = 53   Mean = 6.5   Std. dev. = 1.83

Value	Freq.	%	0...1...2...3...4...5...6...7...8...9...0
10	4	7.5	****
9	0	0.0	
8	15	28.3	**********
7	3	5.7	***
6	20	37.7	**************
5	3	5.7	***
4	6	11.3	******
3	0	0.0	
2	2	3.8	**
1	0	0.0	

Personal and confidential
Urgent: Return by

MANAGEMENT SEMINAR FOLLOW-UP SURVEY

Code: _____

Participants' supervisors' form

XYZ is engaged in a comprehensive study of all of its management development. This questionnaire asks you to report on the effectiveness of the management seminar for one of your subordinates. _____ attended the seminar during _____ Reflect on how he/she was performing before and after the seminar and fill out this survey on how the seminar affected this manager's performance. You will be asked to make suggestions for improving the management seminar. If you receive more than one of these questionnaires, write suggestions on only one copy.

It is important that you be candid in this assessment, since your data will be used to improve the seminars we shall be conducting in the coming months. This questionnaire is coded, but your responses will be pooled with others' to study patterns and trends. You will not be individually identifiable in the analysis of the data.

Use this ten-point scale for your responses:

10	To a very great extent
8	To a great extent
6	To some extent
4	To a little extent
2	To a very little extent

You may use in-between (odd) numbers as well, but do not use zero. Write the number at the end of each of the following items. Then return this form in the enclosed envelope.

To what extent did the management seminar have a beneficial effect on this manager in the following areas? Leave blank those areas that do not apply to this person's job.

1   Affirmative action and equal employment opportunity   ☐
2   Safety   ☐
3   Managing employee benefits   ☐
4   Appraisal interviewing   ☐
5   Budgeting and accounting   ☐
6   Estimating   ☐
7   Order entry   ☐
8   Conference leadership   ☐
9   Operations   ☐
10 Interviewing, testing and hiring   ☐
11 Labour relations   ☐
12 Reading and interpreting manufacturing reports   ☐
13 Quality control procedures   ☐
14 To what extent did the management seminar increase his/her confidence as a manager?   ☐
15 To what degree did this person's attendance at the seminar boost his/her morale?   ☐
16 To what extent did his/her going to the seminar create a better feeling for working at XYZ?   ☐
17 To what extent did the seminar make this person more proud of the XYZ product?   ☐
18 To what degree did the seminar increase his/her loyalty to XYZ?   ☐
19 To what degree did participation in the seminar generate increased overall effectiveness as a manager for this person?   ☐
20 To what degree has the improvement in this person's performance persisted since the training?   ☐

Suggestions for improving the management seminar:

Return this questionnaire to:
Director, Management Development,
XYZ Corporate Headquarters.

Thank you for your co-operation in this important study.

XYZ ORGANISATION MANAGEMENT SEMINAR SURVEY

Supervisors = 54

Affirmative action, equal employment opportunity

Item 1   Respondents = 25   Mean = 5.6   Std. dev. = 1.98

Value	Freq.	%	0...1...2...3...4...5...6...7...8...9...0
10	0	0.0	
9	0	0.0	
8	4	16.0	*******
7	5	20.0	********
6	8	32.0	************
5	1	4.0	**
4	3	12.0	******
3	0	0.0	
2	4	16.0	*******
1	0	0.0	

Safety

Item 2   Respondents = 39   Mean = 5.2   Std. dev. = 1.98

Value	Freq.	%	0...1...2...3...4...5...6...7...8...9...0
10	1	2.6	*
9	0	0.0	
8	4	10.3	*****
7	4	10.3	*****
6	11	28.2	**********
5	4	10.3	*****
4	9	23.1	********
3	0	0.0	
2	6	15.4	******
1	0	0.0	

Managing employee benefits

Item 3   Respondents = 34   Mean = 5.5   Std. dev. = 1.91

Value	Freq.	%	0...1...2...3...4...5...6...7...8...9...0
10	0	0.0	
9	0	0.0	
8	8	23.5	**********
7	2	5.9	***
6	8	23.5	**********
5	3	8.8	***
4	9	26.5	**********
3	1	2.9	*
2	3	8.8	****
1	0	0.0	